Myths on the Margins

Myths on the Margins

Making It to the Center

William Loader

CASCADE *Books* · Eugene, Oregon

MYTHS ON THE MARGINS
Making It to the Center

Cascade Books
An Imprint of Wipf and Stock Publishers
199 W. 8th Ave., Suite 3
Eugene, OR 97401

www.wipfandstock.com

PAPERBACK ISBN: 978-1-6667-3584-0
HARDCOVER ISBN: 978-1-6667-9340-6
EBOOK ISBN: 978-1-6667-9341-3

Cataloguing-in-Publication data:

Names: Loader, William R. G., 1944–, author.

Title: Myths on the margins : making it to the center / William Loader.

Description: Eugene, OR: Cascade Books, 2022. | Includes bibliographical references.

Identifiers: ISBN 978-1-6667-3584-0 (paperback). | ISBN 978-1-6667-9340-6 (hardcover). | ISBN 978-1-6667-9341-3 (ebook).

Subjects: LCSH: Myth in the Bible. | Myth in the Old Testament. | Myth in the New Testament | Bible. Genesis—Myths.

Classification: BS1183 L63 2022 (print). | BS1183 (ebook).

09/15/22

Contents

Preface

ARE YOU INQUISITIVE? THEN myths are for you. In the world of the Bible myths were an early form of science, explaining why things are the way they are. A child may ask: "Where do rainbows come from?" An adult might have asked: "Why is there so much suffering in the world?" Answers came in the form of mythical stories.

The wise sages who assembled the stories of Israel's forbears in the first book of the Bible, Genesis, introduced their collection with the retelling of such myths. If we know Genesis, we know them well: the story of how man and woman were made, the adventures of Adam and Eve, the origins of death and pain and poor soil, and why we wear clothes, not to speak of the Tower of Babel and the story of Noah and the great flood.

Science now offers more informed answers for many such questions. We know what makes rainbows and we know that the universe has been expanding and evolving for thirteen and half billion years, not just the six thousand years which Bible genealogies, when added up, suggest. For some, "myth" is a derogatory term for what you shouldn't believe. "It's a myth" means "It's false." For others, including my inquisitive mind, myths can be both false and true, sometimes profoundly true. Did different languages develop among humankind because God or the gods disapproved of their constructing a skyscraper at Babel to make a name for themselves and sent it crashing down scattering them across the earth? Of course not. But did their wanting to make a name for themselves produce a major communication breakdown? Truly it did and does.

This book is about myths and how they work, but is more specifically about some less well-known myths which made it to the center of faith or nearly did. Do you know about the angels who mated with human women?

What about the rulers who presented themselves as God's second in charge, as God's adopted sons, or even as gods, themselves? And do you know about Woman Wisdom who walked the streets calling men to enter her house and enjoy her love? And can you imagine a family squabble in the heavenly family of gods which led one to go off in a huff and create the world, trapping divine light in its sinister physical, material substances?

The idea for this book came from a series I ran at the Wembley Downs Uniting Church, in Perth, Western Australia, with the same name. One of those who read earlier drafts is its pastor, Karen Sloan. I am grateful to her and to my other readers, Sharyn Robinson, Dr. Robyn Whitaker, and my wife, Gisela, for their feedback.

I have sought to stay close to the ancient sources, preferring to cite them directly rather than simply summarize. A list of translations of those ancient sources which I have cited comes after the final chapter.

This book is about these myths and how all but the last made it in refined form into the heart of faith. It begins, however, first with the familiar Genesis myths and imagines their role in a family discussion set off by a boy treading on a dastardly prickle.

William Loader

1

Myths We All Know

THIS CHAPTER LISTENS IN to a family conversation, imagined as typical of how the myths we all know might function in matters of everyday life. As such it functions as a reminder of the familiar before we venture in following chapters towards the unfamiliar. I invite you to use your imagination.

～ ～ ～

"Ouch! A prickle! Why did God make prickles?"

Seven-year-old Brian was examining the sole of his right foot.

His grandmother smiled and replied: "Brian, let me tell you a story."

She was fond of telling stories.

"One day a very long time ago there were just two people on earth, Adam and Eve, and they lived in a garden which God planted. There was plenty for them to eat but God told them not to eat the fruit from one of the trees in the middle of the garden. They did, and God got angry and threw them out of the garden and punished them. One of the punishments was that he made plants with prickles and thorns."

"And more than that," piped up Helen, Brian's sister. "God made some of the soil infertile and told them they would not live forever but get old and die and lots more."

Brian's father could not resist adding: "Yes, and that women should be subject to their husbands in all things!"

Gwen, Brian's mother laughed.

"You don't really believe all that, do you?" said Helen. She loved doing science at school. "All mammals die. It's natural. Prickles and thorns are just the way some plants have evolved. Soils can be fertile or infertile depending on where they are. Alluvial soils in valleys are rich and fertile.

Those on slopes leached by rain can be infertile and farms which have been overgrazed can become pretty barren, too. There weren't two people in a garden. Human beings evolved over millions of years . . . "

Helen was in full swing.

"Wait a minute," intervened Grandma. "I wasn't saying these stories are all true. They are ancient stories people used to explain why things are the way they are. They're not science, but they can still tell us something. The Adam and Eve myth was a way of saying things go wrong when you overstep the boundaries, like they did in the story."

Kevin, Brian's dad, was in a mischievous mood. "The only bit that's still true is that women should obey men!"

"Now you're being silly," Gwen, his wife, replied. "But, you know, that myth had a big influence. They explained why things were the way they were."

Gwen was a teacher at the university and knew a lot about ancient history. "You see," she explained, "back in the cultures where those who wrote the Bible belonged, men usually married around thirty years of age and they married wives who were often just half their age, young teenagers. It was typical that men thought they were superior. They were older and had more life experience and were mostly bigger and stronger, but that didn't mean they were superior. That was a male fallacy that has lasted over the centuries. Women still don't get equal pay for equal work in some places."

Grandma chipped in. "I remember when your Grandad and I got married. I was expected to stay home and do the housework while he went out to work. He was the head of the house, but, you know, he wasn't really. I had to look after the money side and even then, we knew families on farms where men and women did different things but were equal partners. Both worked."

"Both worked in the ancient world, too," added Gwen. "It was only a century or so ago that that changed with the industrial revolution. Especially in cities men went out to work in factories and women stayed home. But let's have a look at your prickle, Brian. Is it still hurting?"

"Yes," said Brian, "but it's not God's fault. Our lawn seems to be full of prickles."

Helen always found conversations with her grandmother and her mum interesting. "So, when Grandad died, that was not because God made him die. He just died. He was old."

"Yes," replied Grandma. "The first chapters of the Bible, in the book of Genesis, have lots of stories about why things are the way they are, myths. They used the Adam and Eve story to explain why people wear clothes, especially to cover their private parts, and to explain why there are two kinds of people, male and female, men and women. Originally there was just a man and then God conducted an operation and made a woman from one of his ribs. And there are two stories about how God made the man. One tells how God made the man as the last of all of the works of creation on the sixth day and the other has God make a clay model and breathe on it, bringing it to life and only then made plants and animals."

"But you don't believe all those things, do you, gran?" replied Helen.

Her mum was in the middle of an operation on Brian's foot to extract the prickle but couldn't help herself. "You see, people made up stories to explain the way things were. Women were inferior, they thought, so it all had to start with a man! At least the story indicates that God thought making women was a good thing. Plato thought women came about because some men failed and so in their next life—he believed in such things—they came back as women and if they failed, they would next come back as animals, and so on, all the way down to being snakes on the ground."

"Ouch!"

"Sorry, Brian," said Gwen. "The needle slipped. Some of these topics are really just like thorns, too. So, I get a bit angry."

Helen wanted to know more. "Gran, in your old Bible there's a date given on the first page for the first day of creation: 4004 BC. That's just over six thousand years ago, but we know the universe is just over 13.5 billion years old."

"That's simply a bit of arithmetic, Helen," replied her gran. "You add up all the ages of people in the Old Testament of the Bible right back to Adam and Eve and you get to around that figure. It's the same with the seven days. People in those ancient times told these stories to explain things. Why are there seven days? Why keep the seventh day as a day of rest? How were animals and plants created? It's rather funny because the story starts with a day before there could have been a day because God hadn't yet created the sun. The truth behind all these stories is that behind everything is God, not some evil power and not just nothing and that creation as it has evolved over billions of years is something good, including men and, of course, women!"

By this time Gwen had finished, having extracted the prickle. "You could hardly see it. Almost nothing."

"But it hurt!" Brian responded.

"Yes, of course," said his mum, who went on: "Little things can have such a big impact. Those ancient myths talk about consequences. That's why people told them. Don't be like Adam and Eve! Know your limitations."

Helen was keen to move on: "So the story about Noah was their explanation about how rainbows were made and the story about the Tower of Babel which people built to make a name for themselves was to explain why there are different languages when God scattered them over the earth."

"Yes," replied her grandmother. "Communication between people breaks down when they are bent on making a name for themselves. That's the deeper meaning. These are myths with meaning. In that sense they are really true."

It was time for bed and when all was settled and Gwen, Kevin, and Gran were just on their own, Gwen returned to the theme. "Wasn't that interesting?" she said. "There's quite a bit more, especially the way people in New Testament times read these stories. They read them in the Greek translation of the Old Testament not the original Hebrew. Translations do things to texts. When Eve explains to God that the snake "tricked" her into eating the forbidden fruit, the Greek uses a word which, unlike the Hebrew, can mean "seduced," sexually. So, people like Paul were reading it that way. Moral of the story: women can be easily sexually seduced."

"And seduce others," added Kevin with a smile.

"Well, indeed, that was their view," Gwen replied. "Men saw women as less able to control their emotions and so told themselves that women need to be kept under strict control, daughters until they were married and wives when they were married. Women were not to be trusted. That meant they were not suitable for leadership and for centuries were banned from leadership in the church and still are in some churches. There were exceptions then, especially because many who had become Jesus' followers were at the bottom of the heap in society and so felt equal, equally disadvantaged. So not surprisingly some women emerged among them as leaders beside the men—at least for a time unto the movement became respectable."

"I'm not being silly," commented Kevin, "but they really do seem to have been afraid of women. Jesus' saying about looking at a woman and finding her attractive as being like committing adultery is a bit extreme.

No wonder they insisted on covering them up. They were a liability for any good man. Sex is obviously a bad thing for men!"

"Not so hasty, Kevin," answered Gwen. "The saying of Jesus has been read in that way, but the Greek original is better understood as saying that men who lust after others' wives wanting to have sex with them are adulterers in their heart, in their minds, and so need to take responsibility for their sexuality. Sex was not seen as something bad but as something which like their other appetites needed to be controlled. As Matthew portrays it, Jesus was telling men to take control of themselves and used extreme imagery to do so, suggesting they figuratively cut off the limbs that offend."

"It's interesting that the Adam and Eve story attributes pain in childbirth to punishment for their sin," added the grandmother.

"Human females have trouble giving birth because the species has had a narrow birth canal even since we dropped down out of the trees and walked upright in the savannah, resulting in the narrowing of the hips," observed Kevin. "We can't do the finished product like other mammals."

"That little list of curses on humankind," commented Gwen, "comes through in Greek translation as saying that women are forever wanting to have sex with their husbands and so forever becoming pregnant. The translators also created more inequality by matching the creation of woman to the creation of man so that as man, according to the story, was made in the image of God, so woman was made in the image or likeness of the man. In the story the sexual impulse derives from the two parts of the original human, the male and female, wanting to re-join, a fascinating theory of origin. That element of the story is depicting sexual desire as connection and intimacy in contrast or alongside what we find in the first creation account where sex is about obeying the command given to both humans and animals to multiply."

"Things have changed a lot over my lifetime," Gran mused. "We got married just when effective contraception became available and since then there has been a revolution in the roles of women and men. We need a whole new set of myths. Now both can be free to exercise leadership in the family, in the community, indeed, in the world."

"Not talking about the good old days, Nan?" quipped Kevin. "It seems like some of these myths were doing that. Remember paradise, human beings? What went wrong? People do have fantasies about the old days which sometimes match reality and sometimes don't. One of the ways of coming to terms with loss is to explain why it is so. These say there was paradise and we lost it and it is Adam and Eve's and in a sense God's fault. In some ways this is not facing reality. God isn't controlling everything like that. There is loss. There are prickles! God walks on our lawn, too!"

"I think we ought to treasure these myths," reflected Gwen. "They are gifts of ancient culture to us. They are all untrue and all true at the same time. God is why there is not just nothing. Creation is an evolving reality, a mystery, but not something evil. Men and women are good and equal in their differences. They can stuff up and there are consequences, and these can last across generations, just as soil can be degraded for decades. We need myths to tell us about climate change and what we are doing. The claim of the Christian story was another myth, if you like, life out of death, new beginnings. It was grounded in the cluster of stories about Jesus who expounded his Jewish heritage to give us a universal story of hope and love. We need myths to live by because in some ways fantasy is our way to reality like the sound which words make is our way to meaning."

꿁 꿁 꿁

That conversation ended. They were reflecting on myths still central to the faith of so many, Jews, Christians, Muslims. The following chapters turn to myths which also impacted the people of faith's beginnings as reflected in the writings of the Bible but did so more from the margins.

2

The Myth of the Wicked Angels

MOST OF THE MYTHS or stories found in the first chapters of Genesis are well known, from the story of Noah and the Tower of Babel, back to the garden of Eden and Adam and Eve. Much less well known is the myth of the wicked angels mentioned only very briefly in Genesis 6. It begins in the first two verses: "When people began to multiply on the face of the ground, and daughters were born to them, ²the sons of God saw that they were fair; and they took wives for themselves of all that they chose" (Genesis 6:1–2). The story returns and concludes in verse 4: "The Nephilim were on the earth in those days—and also afterwards—when the sons of God went in to the daughters of humans, who bore children to them. These were the heroes that were of old, warriors of renown" (Genesis 6:4).

There is much more to this story than is touched upon in these brief references and even these need some explanation. The "sons of God" was a way of referring to angels. They were not literally children of God. There was room for confusion because the Hebrew word for God, *Elohim*, was also a word for angels and divine or heavenly beings. Most probably the background for this is that Israel's God, YHWH, was seen in earlier times not as the only god but as the chief of the gods, at least in some circles. When Israel came to claim there is only one God and that that God is YHWH, then the other gods, though still called *Elohim* (gods), were demoted and relegated to the status of angels or at least as inferior beings. Angels could be called "sons of God." Angels were sons because they were all assumed to be male. Occasionally we find other references to them as angels or gods, such as in Psalm 82, where the psalmist declares, "God has taken his place in the divine council; in the midst of the gods he holds judgement" (Psalm 82:1). The "divine council" was like a supreme court or assembly of at least the most important gods or angels. The book of Job reports, for instance, a conversation when the "sons of God," angels, convened. One of them called, "Satan," whose name means "the prosecutor or accuser," mounted a case against Job, asking that he might put him to the test to see if he really was so righteous as his reputation suggested. God acceded to his request and so commissioned him to do so (Job 2:1–6). Similarly in Zechariah we read that the high priest Joshua stood before God along with Satan who was making a case against him (Zechariah 3:1–2).

The idea of a divine supreme court continued right through into New Testament times when we find, for instance, Paul writing that if believers are accused before God they would have a defense attorney, namely Jesus, who would speak on their behalf. Thus, he writes in his letter to the Romans: "Who will bring any charge against God's elect? It is God who justifies. [34]Who is to condemn? It is Christ Jesus, who died, yes, who was raised, who is at the right hand of God, who indeed intercedes for us" (Romans 8:33–34). Similarly, the author of 1 John speaks of Jesus in this role: "My little children, I am writing these things to you so that you may not sin. But if anyone does sin, we have an advocate with the Father, Jesus Christ the righteous; [2]and he is the atoning sacrifice for our sins, and not for ours only but also for the sins of the whole world" (1 John 2:1–2). People came to speak of angels also as powers which God controls and sends on missions. In Hebrews the author cites Psalm 104:4 in a form that speaks of angels: "He makes his angels winds and his servants flames of fire" (Hebrews 1:7) and adds in 1:14, "Are not all angels spirits in the divine service, sent to serve for the sake of those who are to inherit salvation?" Our word "angel" comes from a Greek word which can simply mean "messenger," reflecting the more usual Hebrew word for angels which means a "sent one." Over time people came to speak of angels as God's messengers or servants.

Sometimes, instead of speaking of God coming to people, they spoke of the "Angel of the LORD." And the more that people thought of God as holy and remote, the more they would see angels as bridging the gap. They imagined angels in charge of the weather, intervening in human affairs on God's behalf, delivering the ten commandments to Moses and being guardians or sponsors of people on earth, such as when we read of people and especially children as having guardian angels. Matthew has Jesus warn against child abuse with reference to such angels: "Take care that you do not despise one of these little ones; for, I tell you, in heaven their angels continually see the face of my Father in heaven" (18:10). In the Christmas story we read of the angel Gabriel visiting Mary. They are sometimes called the "watchers" because they watch over all that is happening on God's behalf.

In some circles people thought about each nation as having an angel that looked after them. YHWH, in that sense, was the god who looked after Israel's interests. You can imagine that when conflict took place between nations, they could see this as conflict between the gods or angels of the nations. It was common to imagine the heavenly world as full of angels. This continues through into New Testament times and beyond. The book of Revelation pictures heaven as like a temple with angels constantly engaged in worship. When people spoke of Jesus' coming again, it was often that he would be accompanied by angels. Thus, in Mark we read of the end times: "Then they will see 'the Son of Man coming in clouds' with great power and glory. [27]Then he will send out the angels, and gather his elect from the four winds, from the ends of the earth to the ends of heaven" (Mark 13:26). Generally, people thought of angels as good. We can imagine, however, that the guardian angels of foreign nations would not always be seen in a good light. The angel, Satan, is a special case. He was thought of as a member of the heavenly supreme court with a valid role to play as chief prosecutor. As already noted, God even gave him a commission to go out and test Job on God's behalf. Over time this angel got a bad reputation and stories developed which told of his dismissal and being thrown out of the heavenly realm along with the angels which supported him. That is a story in itself which people used to explain chaos on earth.

Equally influential in explaining such chaos, if not more, however, was the myth of the wicked angels or watchers, which, as we have seen, leaves some traces in Genesis 6. In this chapter we shall look at this myth, especially the way it came to be used and re-used over and over again to help people come to terms with what was happening around them.

First, we return to the detail in Genesis 6. It tells us that "sons of God" found human women attractive, took some of them as wives, and bore children by them. There are some basic assumptions even behind these details. The first is that angels are male as we have noted. Why? Because people (men!) thought they were superior to women and so, if angels were superior to them, they would have to be male, too. It is of course a delusion and based on a male delusion about men.

These male angels found human women sexually attractive—as, it is assumed, male humans would. No judgement is made about this in the text. They "take" the women as wives. This language is not uncommon. It would usually assume the normal pattern of having a marriage arranged by negotiation with their fathers. Nothing like this is indicated, so that it sounds more like abduction or rape, also not uncommon in the ancient world. Again, the text passes no judgement. The primary focus in the taking is sex: they engaged in sexual intercourse with these women who became pregnant and gave birth to hybrid creatures: "Nephilim," a word for giants.

The almost incidental comment in the text that these giants became "heroes" and "warriors of renown" may indicate that these events were above board and approved or that the story originated as explanation for their existence. We find a reference to such Nephilim/giants also in the book of Numbers, where it is used to describe people of very large stature (13:33). Again, no judgement is made in the text in Genesis, so that it is possible to read these events as something that was acceptable. Many cultures had legends about giants and such stories may well find their origins in fantasies of little children about the giants which surround their beginnings, especially when their experience with adults had been frightening. Giants can feature as cruel or kind.

Most who heard these references in Genesis 6 in the time they were written would know the full story of the myth and would know that what happened was anything but acceptable. It comes in Genesis in the lead up to the story of Noah, so that, reading between the lines, the world's wickedness which occasioned the flood had been in part set in motion by these wayward angels. Their deed was a major breach of the natural order of God's creation, a mixing of species, like bestiality (humans having sex with animals).

It was an act of violence that would lead to disaster. These angels had lusted after human women whom they found attractive and taken them by abduction and rape, producing monsters capable of wreaking havoc. They would, accordingly, have seen a connection between this story and what followed, namely that wickedness spread over the earth and God had to send a flood to drown it out and saved only Noah and his family. Such was also the understanding of the more elaborate form of the myth which we find elsewhere.

Telling the Whole Story in 1 Enoch 6–16

We find one of the clearest outlines of the story in a writing called the Book of the Watchers, the first in a collection of writings originally written in

Aramaic and now assembled together as 1 Enoch. The writings are attributed to the patriarch Enoch of whom Genesis says: "Enoch walked with God; then he was no more, because God took him" (5:24). That suggested to some that he did not die but instead went straight into the heavenly realms and from there could provide secret information.

In learned circles people, therefore, found Enoch fascinating. What did he see? Did he see the future? Could he tell us? Some imagined that he could, and this led to writings alleging that they owed their information to Enoch. This was what they imagined. The collection of works in 1 Enoch is attributed in this way to Enoch.

It was not uncommon for authors to attribute their writings to great figures of the past. Already in the Old Testament we find the first five books attributed to Moses, though they include reference to his death. Similarly, people attributed works of wisdom to Solomon and psalms to David. Usually what we now know as prophetic books, contain both material spoken by the prophet as well as material from others usually spoken in deference to the prophet, even some centuries later. The trend continued and the collection in 1 Enoch is a good example of it.

Until recent decades, we knew of 1 Enoch mainly from copies used by the church in Ethiopia, where it belongs to their Scripture. Until recently our main sources were complete copies of 1 Enoch in the Ethiopic Geʻez language and also extensive extracts from it in Greek, Latin, and a few other languages. Then much older copies of three of the five writings in the collection came to light among the scrolls hidden in the caves by the Dead Sea at Qumran. They were preserved in their original language, Aramaic, and included the Book of the Watchers. These recent finds confirm that three of the writings in 1 Enoch come from at least as early as the first century BCE.

The first in the collection, the Book of the Watchers, appears to be the oldest. It is, itself, a work which has various layers, some going back to at least the late fourth century BCE. These writings came from the learned people of their day as they reflected further on the story found in Genesis. Not many people had the skills and training to be able to write and most belonged to priestly circles.

The Story according to 1 Enoch 6–11

The simplest version of the story of the watchers belongs to these very early layers and is found in 1 Enoch 6–11. Here it is in outline.

It begins, as in Genesis 6, with reference to human beings multiplying on earth and similarly adds: "beautiful and comely daughters were born to them. And the watchers, the sons of heaven, saw them and desired them. And they said to one another, 'Come, let us choose for ourselves wives from the daughters of men, and let us beget children for ourselves'" (1 Enoch 6:1–2). One of the watchers, Shemihazah, their leader, challenged them to join him in doing so and they agreed, swearing an oath that they would do so. The story goes on to say that two hundred of them descended onto the peak of Mount Hermon. It names their top twenty leaders, beginning with Shemihazah: "These and all the others with them took for themselves wives from among them such as they chose. And they began to go into them, and to defile themselves through them, and to teach them sorcery and charms, and to reveal to them the cutting roots and plants" (1 Enoch 7:1). We shall come back to what they taught, but first the story continues. "And they conceived from them and bore to them great giants" (1 Enoch 7:2). These created havoc on earth. "They were devouring the labor of all the sons of man, and men were not able to supply them. And the giants began to kill men and devour them" (1 Enoch 7:3–4).

Then, according to the story, the angels, Michael, Sariel, Raphael, and Gabriel, seeing what was happening and hearing humanity's cries, approached God for help for humanity (1 Enoch 9). In response, God told Sariel to instruct Noah to get ready for a flood to wipe out all the evil (1 Enoch 10:1–3). He told Raphael to bind Asael, one of the leading watchers, in darkness until the judgement day and its conflagration (1 Enoch 10:4–8). He told Gabriel to go to the giants and "send them against one another in a war of destruction" (1 Enoch 10:9–10) and he told Michael to bind Shemihazah and the rest, have them see the destruction of their hybrid children, the giants, and then confine them in the "fiery abyss" (1 Enoch 10:11–15). This would "destroy all perversity from the face of the earth" (1 Enoch 10:16) and let the righteous live in peace and prosperity (1 Enoch 10:16—11:2).

We come back to the second aspect of the watchers' wicked deeds: their teaching. This is a strand of the story which may well come from a different tradition or version of the story. Its main figure is not Shemihazah but Asael, listed in the main story as one of his subordinates. Thus, there appears to have been a separate story where Asael was the main actor. It is now woven into the main story in 1 Enoch 8. Asael was, accordingly, responsible for passing on dangerous information: "Asael taught men to make swords of iron and weapons and shields and breastplates and every instrument of war. He showed them metals of the earth and how they should work gold to fashion it suitably, and concerning silver, to fashion it for bracelets and ornaments of women. And he showed them concerning antimony and eye paint and all manner of precious stones and dyes" (1 Enoch 8:1). Thus, the watchers taught metallurgy, enhancing weapons of war and creating jewelry for women. This, indeed, enhanced their seductiveness, seen as something evil, indeed making them responsible for seducing the watchers: "they transgressed and led the holy ones astray" (1 Enoch 8:1). Connecting this strand to the main story leads to blaming women for the watchers' sin, typical across the ages of men blaming women and their sexuality. It also might imply that Asael descended before Shemihazah and his 200 because it was his teaching which enhanced the attractiveness of the women, as in some later versions of the myth, although that is not explicit here. Merging the strand with the main story, the storyteller goes on to list what each of the other leading angels in the main story taught, from spells and sorcery to astrology (1 Enoch 8:3).

Chapters 6–11 thus depict the main story of the watchers' sin, their sexual engagement with women and the birth of giants who created chaos and finally slaughtered each other. The wickedness also included the watchers' teaching men metallurgy and the women sorcery, witchcraft, and the implements of seduction, evils to be destroyed from the face of the earth.

The Story in 1 Enoch 12–16

In 1 Enoch 12–16, the section which follows in the Book of the Watchers, we see further developments of the main story. The story is now told on the lips of Enoch, himself. Enoch was not even mentioned in chapters 6–11 but he was introduced in chapter 1 as the source of the information to follow.

It is therefore not surprising that we find that this next section of the Book of the Watchers, chapters 12–16, is portrayed as information stemming from Enoch. According to this development of the story, the good angels told Enoch to tell the wicked watchers that they would never be forgiven and that they must suffer the pain of watching their children self-destruct in mutual warfare (1 Enoch 12:3–6). He was told also to reprimand Asael, in particular, and then all of them (1 Enoch 13:1–3).

The wicked angels, in response, asked Enoch to speak to God on their behalf to ask for mercy (1 Enoch 13:4). In a series of visions which follow, we read of Enoch approaching God with their petition and God refusing it. Enoch then reports this to the wicked watchers, telling them that from then on, they would be banned from heaven, would have to see their hybrid offspring kill each other and would then be bound and taken prisoner (1 Enoch 13:8—14:23).

In one of these visions Enoch was taken up into heaven and saw God's lofty throne (1 Enoch 14:8–23). "Flaming fire encircled him and a great fire stood by him, and none of those about him approached him. Ten thousand times ten thousand stood before him" (1 Enoch 14:22). God then gave Enoch instructions about what he should say to the wicked watchers. It included: "Why have you forsaken the high heaven, the eternal sanctuary; and lain with women, and defiled yourselves with the daughters of men; and taken for yourselves wives, and done as the sons of earth; and begotten for yourselves sons, giants?" (1 Enoch 15:3). Already the reference to "sanctuary" suggests that they served as priests in the sanctuary of heaven. Sexual intercourse rendered priests ritually unclean until the next day and they had performed ablutions. Such ritual defilement was not, itself, sinful. Temple priests were usually married so this was standard procedure. Ritual impurity was about what was and what was not allowed in sacred space. In the same way women menstruating or having given birth were "unclean" for a time. This had nothing to do with sin. In the case of the watchers as priests of heaven, they defiled themselves ritually, but what was much more serious was that they also defiled themselves morally by breaking divine law, engaging in sex beyond their own species.

The reprimand continues with further explanation, referring to humans as "flesh and blood, who die and perish" (1 Enoch 15:4), and explaining, "Therefore I gave them women, that they might cast seed into them, and thus beget children by them, that nothing fail them on the earth. But you originally existed as spirits, living forever, and not dying for all generations of eternity; therefore I did not make women among you" (1 Enoch 15:4-7). This explanation carries some key assumptions. One is the widespread and quaint understanding about how human reproduction works. Men cast seed into women, who like rich soil nurture it to birth. We now know that the seed or egg is already in the woman and that male sperm fertilizes it.

The second flawed assumption in this explanation, sometimes but not always found in writings of the period, is that sexual intercourse has one function only, reproduction, and has no place apart from that, ignoring that it might be a way of expressing intimate love and companionship. That is why the story says that since angels live forever, they do not need to reproduce and therefore they do not need to engage in sexual intercourse and so do not need women. We find Luke reflecting this view when he supplements Mark's version of Jesus' words that in the age to come people will neither marry nor be given in marriage because they will be like the angels in heaven (namely in sacred space and of different nature). For he adds: "because they cannot die anymore" (20:36) and, by implication, should not engage in sexual intercourse because human reproduction is no longer needed, assuming engagement in sexual intercourse has only reproduction as its purpose.

Such assumptions lead to the view that allows sexual intercourse only for the purpose of procreation and frowns therefore on sex during menstruation, pregnancy or with contraception. It also implied that in the end women are in that sense superfluous and are best transformed to become the higher form of the species, namely male. Indeed, the Gospel of Thomas, composed in the second century CE, imagines Jesus declaring of Mary: "Lo, I shall lead her, so that I may make her a male, that she too may become a living spirit resembling you males. For every woman who makes herself a male will enter the kingdom of heaven" (Gospel of Thomas0 114).

The story in 1 Enoch goes on to have God declare that out of the corpses of the giants, who exterminated themselves through internecine warfare, evil spirits would emerge (1 Enoch 15:9–11). Accordingly, the passage has God declare: "And these spirits of the giants will lead astray, do violence, make desolate, and attack and wrestle and hurl upon the earth and cause illnesses. . . . These spirits will rise up against the sons of men and against the women, for they have come forth from them . . . they are making desolate without incurring judgment. Thus they will make desolate until the day of the consummation of the great judgment" (1 Enoch 15:11; 16:1). A more literal translation by Eibert Tigchelaar in his book *Prophets of Old and the Day of the End: Zechariah, the Book of Watchers and Apocalyptic* brings out the fact that these descriptions are more to be seen as labels or names of different kinds of evil spirits: "The spirits of the giants are Afflicters (or: lurkers), Smiters, Destroyers, Assailants, Strikers, Earth Demons, and Crushers."[1] He notes also that the list of seven names matches the number of seven demons used frequently in Mesopotamian incantation spells.

1. Tigchelaar, *Prophets of Old*, 204.

These spirits set out to bring harm to human beings, probably envisaging all kinds of physical and mental afflictions.

Reviewing the Story in 1 Enoch 6–16

The main story in 1 Enoch 6–16, simply put, is that some angels found women attractive, came down from the heavens, took them as their wives, and had sexual relations with them. The women conceived and gave birth to giants. The giants ended up fighting one another to death and out of their corpses came evil spirits which now bring harm to humans, causing all kinds of illness physical and mental.

Why was it important as a myth? Like most myths, it explained why things are the way they are. In this instance, it explained what makes people sick. In some ways it was an advance in science because it identified that there were forces out there in the world which produced illness. We might call such things viruses or bacteria. They personalized them. This was an alternative to seeing adverse experiences such as illness as God's work or necessarily one's own fault. It was in that sense a move away from strict theism where people believed that God controlled everything. Instead, there were random forces at play. It was in that sense an advance in knowledge and understanding of reality.

Belief in spirits and demons was of course widespread in the cultures of the day but this myth explained their origin. It had significant influence. We read little of evil spirits in the Old Testament but in the New Testament such spirits take center stage. Gospel writers like Luke saw almost all sickness as produced by such evil spirits, sometimes called demons or unclean spirits. Typically, he rewrites Mark's account of Jesus' healing of Peter's mother-in-law, changing "He came and took her by the hand and lifted her up. Then the fever left her, and she began to serve them" (Mark 1:31) to "Then he stood over her and rebuked the fever, and it left her. Immediately she got up and began to serve them" (Luke 4:39). Luke turned it into an exorcism. Jesus rebuked the fever.

It was possible to see nearly every act of healing as an exorcism, that is, an expulsion of evil spirits or a loosening of their hold on people. Mental illness in particular seemed best explained by evil spirits, being possessed by a demon or demons, especially when people acted out of character as they frequently do in schizophrenic or psychotic episodes.

Applying the Story within its Retelling in 1 Enoch 6–16

Myths generate meanings and stimulate reflection. In the case of the main story, we see traces in 1 Enoch 6–16 of people taking it and applying it to their own day. The exploitation and devastation wrought on earth by the marauding giants and their wars appear to have inspired some to see in them a prefiguring of what happened after Alexander the Great's unexpected death in his early thirties in 323 BCE. He had marched in conquest with his army from Macedon in Greece as far as India only to fall ill and die young. In the years that followed, 323–302 BCE, his generals fought each other, leading to devastation and exploitation for many of the people in northern Israel and Syria. In this way the myth provided a pattern for their reflection. What happened in the myth was happening again!

Another generation found that the story helped them address a problem which arose when priests married outside of the strictly defined limits imposed on them, especially when they married foreigners. Josephus, the late-first-century CE Jewish historian, reports the controversial marriage of Manasseh, brother of the high priest Jaddua, to Nikaso, daughter of the Samaritan Sanballat, and notes that other priests did similarly (*A.J.* 11). Like the angels, whose role was to remain priests in the heavenly sanctuary, these men who, differently from the angels, were permitted to marry within limits, went beyond those limits and this, they argued, produced defilement of the temple and subsequent disaster for all Jews.

Whether it was priests not keeping to their rules or ordinary Israelites marrying foreigners, the result was in the eyes of many: pollution. There was prejudice against foreigners and especially against foreign women amongst some. For foreign women were allegedly bearers of secret knowledge about how to make spells and practice witchcraft. The myth explained that it was the wicked watchers who had taught women such evil tricks. It now served to reinforce the prohibitions about intermarriage with outsiders for all Jews.

As mentioned earlier, the myth of the watchers led others to see women in general as dangerous because of their sexual attractiveness. They posed a danger, it was alleged, to men by their use of jewelry and cosmetics taught to them by the wicked watchers. They should, therefore, be controlled. Women were to blame when men went wrong. Control them. Cover them up!

The Greek translation of the story of Adam and Eve in Genesis also contributed to negative stereotypes about women. It has Eve declare, "The snake deceived/seduced me" (Genesis 3:13). The Hebrew word behind "deceived" meant "tricked." Unlike the word used by the Greek translator, it did not also mean "seduced." Inevitably, therefore, many who used the Greek translation of Genesis read it as implying that Eve was sexually seduced. Paul assumes this meaning when he writes to the Corinthians that he does not want them to be seduced like Eve but to present them as a pure virgin to Christ at his coming (2 Corinthians 11:2–3). The watcher myth reinforced this notion of women as seductive and easily seduced.

The myth of the watchers served to underline the importance of not crossing forbidden boundaries, especially sexual boundaries, and to emphasize that when you do, disaster follows. This had also been the message of the story of Adam and Eve and the forbidden fruit. Both stories serve therefore not just as explanations of why things went wrong and are the way they are, but also as warnings, in the case of the watcher myth, especially in the area of sexual behavior. The watcher myth helped people see their own disasters, like sickness and mental illness in new ways.

Retellings of the Story

The Animal Apocalypse in the Book
of Dream Visions (1 Enoch 83–90)

One of the other writings incorporated into the collection called 1 Enoch is the Book of Dream Visions (1 Enoch 83–90), written probably early to mid-second century BCE. Most of it is taken up with what is called the Animal Apocalypse (1 Enoch 85–90), a dream portraying the history of humanity using the imagery of animals. Adam and Eve are a white bull and a young heifer (1 Enoch 85:3). In contrast to Genesis, nothing is said about their sin. The first to sin is Cain who killed Abel, depicted as a black bull which killed a red one (1 Enoch 85:3). The cows bred and soon there was a big herd.

Next, it depicts a star falling from heaven and eating among the cattle (1 Enoch 86:1). It caused confusion among them: "all of them exchanged their pens and their pastures and their calves, and began to moan, one after another" (1 Enoch 86:2). The moaning (mooing?) is probably indicating inappropriate joining behavior, sexual perversion. This first star reflects the descent of Asael in the myth. After this we read, "I saw many stars descend and cast themselves down from heaven . . . in the midst of those calves they became bulls. . . . All of them let out their organs like horses and they began to mount the cows of the bulls and they all conceived and bore elephants and camels and asses and all of the bulls feared and were terrified before them" (1 Enoch 86:3–5). These stars are Shemihazah and his 200 fellow-watchers in the myth. The elephants, camels, and asses are the giants of the myth.

The next part of the vision has these animals fighting each other, as the giants did in the myth (1 Enoch 87:1). They also symbolize foreign nations. In response to this situation, as in the myth, four angels appear as white men and take Enoch (who is reporting his dream) to a tower to watch what happens next (1 Enoch 87:2–4). He sees Asael bound and thrown into the abyss. Then one of the angels gives the wild animals a sword and they engage each other in battle creating havoc. Another of the angels threw stones down on the stars, bound them and threw them, too, into the abyss (1 Enoch 88:1–3).

Next comes the story of Noah and flood. The wild animals and all the wayward bulls drown in the flood. Only a white bull (Noah) survived (1 Enoch 89:1–9). The vision goes on to tell the rest of Israel's history using animal imagery (1 Enoch 89:10—90:38). It includes seeing foreign nations again as wild animals but also seeing Israel as sheep and noting that some sheep were leading others astray. It concludes with judgement day and a vision of hope which includes not only Israel and its renewed temple but also all the nations, all becoming white cattle (1 Enoch 90:37–38), recalling the original creation of Adam as a white bull (1 Enoch 85:3).

The main variation on the myth, apart from the imagery, is that the giants (the wild animals) drown in the flood rather than kill each other in warfare. Another is that there is more clearly a separate descent of Asael before Shemihazah and his two hundred descend. In addition, whereas the main story in 1 Enoch 6–15 has three main stages, the descent of the watchers, the birth of the giants, and the emergence of the evil spirits from their carcasses, the Animal Apocalypse reflects a version of the myth which has two stages: the descent of the angels (stars, in two steps) and the birth of the giants (wild animals). This merges the second and third stages of the main myth because the wild animals are also the evil spirits, especially as they become Israel's enemies. In part, this reflects an understanding that sees them as inspiring the attacks and corrupting influence of foreign nations.

The Book of Jubilees

The book of Jubilees also tells of the descent of the watchers (Jubilees 5:1–12). It was written in Hebrew in the early to mid-second century BCE, around the same time as the Animal Apocalypse. It retells the stories of Genesis and of the first chapters of Exodus, claiming to be what God told Moses through his angel on Mount Sinai when he received the law. Its purpose is to explain how history will develop, setting it out as a series of blocks of fifty years, sometimes called "jubilees," hence its name. It has a special interest in future hope but also in how people should understand and keep God's law and the dangerous consequences if they don't.

It, too, therefore, retells the myth of the wicked angels, as told in Genesis 6 and subsequently elaborated. Its version of the story is slightly different from those considered so far. In its version of the story, the angels came down to earth not because they were wicked, but because God sent them. They had been sent by God down to earth "to teach humankind and to do what is just and upright on the earth" (Jubilees 4:15). Jewish writings often depict angels as teachers or bearers of information. Even the law was given through such angels, as Paul and the writer of Hebrews note (Galatians 3:19; Hebrews 2:3–4).

Teaching was their main task, but it was while they were teaching that they fell into sin. For Jubilees depicts them as finding human women sexually attractive. Unlike in Genesis 6:2 and the myth as developed in the Book of the Watchers, this was not, therefore, because they looked down from heaven and saw them. Rather they were on duty as teachers and in that context made their move, archetypes, alas, of predatory sexual grooming which is still alive and well. Unlike the main story in 1 Enoch 6–15, however, the watchers, themselves, were solely to blame. Women were not to blame. The teachings which the watchers gave had nothing to do with metallurgy, making jewelry or cosmetics, as in the Book of the Watchers. At most, Jubilees tells us that they taught astrology which in one instance, it reports, was still preserved as "an inscription which the ancients had incised in a rock" (Jubilees 8:3–4).

Jubilees' version follows the detail of the women giving birth to giants and that the giants were then set on a path of mutual warfare leading to their demise with their watcher fathers looking on in distress (Jubilees 5:7–10). It reads Genesis 6:3, formulated as a statement about human beings and sitting awkwardly in its context in Genesis, "My spirit will not remain on people forever for they are flesh. Their lifespan is to be 120 years," not as referring to humans but as referring to the giants and their impending demise (Jubilees 5:8). Jubilees, like the Animal Apocalypse, does not have a third stage describing the emergence of evil spirits. Rather it describes the evil spirits as children of the watchers themselves, now mostly bound with them in the abyss.

Furthermore, not all the evil spirits were let loose on humankind to bring them harm. For Noah, it reports, had appealed to God against that prospect and Mastema, the chief of the demons, negotiated (in the heavenly supreme court) that only 10 percent of them be allowed to roam free (Jubilees 17:16). Mastema's negotiation reminds us of Satan's negotiation in Job 2 about the testing of Job. The name Mastema is a variant of the name Satan (*stn/stm*) and means enemy or adversary.

The role of the evil spirits is to inflict harm on human beings, as in the myth in the Book of the Watchers. The author of Jubilees may, however, reflect a less pessimistic stance than what we find there, because he not only has God limit the free-ranging spirits to 10 percent but also has his angels give Noah medical instructions about herbal antidotes (Jubilees 10:10, 12–14). Thus, the angel dictating Jubilees explains, "We told Noah all the medicines for their diseases with their deceptions so that he could cure (them) by means of the earth's plants. Noah wrote down in a book everything (just) as we had taught him regarding all the kinds of medicine" (Jubilees 10:12–13). As in the Animal Apocalypse, Jubilees sees foreign nations as a threat and explains this as something which God allowed, permitting evil spirits to take charge of all the nations except Israel: "He sanctified them and gathered (them) from all mankind. For there are many nations and many peoples and all belong to him. He made spirits rule over all in order to lead them astray from following him. But over Israel he made no angel or spirit rule because he alone is their ruler" (Jubilees 15:31–32). Jubilees also follows later developments of the watcher myth in depicting evil spirits as the inspiration for idolatry (Jubilees 11:4–5; 12:20; 1 Enoch 19:1).

Since Jubilees is a retelling of the book of Genesis and the beginning of Exodus, it knows the other stories used to explain the woes facing humanity. Thus, it tells the story of Adam and Eve and their sin, unlike the Animal Apocalypse. The watchers, therefore, did not, according to Jubilees, invent sin, but it uses their sin as an important basis for understanding all sin.

Above all, Jubilees uses the myth to explain sin, especially sexual sin, in a way that goes beyond what we find in the writings in 1 Enoch where the emphasis on the effects tends to be on the advent of violence and idolatry, apart from the suite of afflictions and illnesses with which the evil spirits plague humankind. Jubilees gives particular attention to sexual sin.

Jubilees emphasizes that sin, and sexual sin in particular, is to cross forbidden boundaries, to go against nature, God's creation. Thus, the watchers' action is a paradigm for what this means. They went against nature by cavorting with human women. Similarly, men go against nature by having sex with animals, bestiality, and, as later authors like Paul see it, men do so also when they have sex with other men, same-gender sexual orientation and behavior (Romans 1:18–32; Testament of Naphtali 3:1–5). All such behavior was seen as abomination (as in Leviticus 20:13; 18:22), given what they assumed to be natural and unnatural. Jubilees' major emphasis on sexual wrongdoing, however, focuses especially on marriage to foreigners.

Further Retellings of the Story

The myth of the watchers, found on the margins, and sketchily portrayed in Genesis 6, exercised widespread influence. In what follows I mention some other writings where we can see the story's influence.

In some the allusions are brief. The book of Judith in the Apocrypha of the Bible, composed early in the first century BCE, makes a connection between the giants and Hellenistic myth of the Titans, equally fearsome monsters from the past (Judith 16:6).

Among the scrolls stored in caves at Qumran by the Dead Sea for safekeeping when the Romans mopped up insurgents in the late 60s CE before retaking Jerusalem in 70 CE are fragments of a writing called the Book of Giants (late third to early second century BCE). It is based on the myth and reflects a form which inculcated both the watchers and the women in the original act of sin. A number of other previously unknown writings found among the scrolls allude to the myth of the angels' sin and its lasting impact through what they frequently describe in terms of disparagement as their half-breed, bastard offspring, evil spirits.

One of the scrolls, called the Genesis Apocryphon, retells the story. It was found in the first cave, hence its abbreviated title, 1Q20/1QapGen (1 = cave 1; Q = Qumran; 20 = document number; apGen = document abbreviation). It was composed at least as early as the first century BCE. It contains an account of the birth of Noah which reflects the influence of the myth. The collection in 1 Enoch has a similar story, in the document called the Birth of Noah (1 Enoch 106–107), probably composed about the same time as the Genesis Apocryphon. In both accounts, Lamech, Noah's father, cannot believe his eyes when he sees the beauty of baby Noah. As the story in the Birth of Noah describes baby Noah, "his body was whiter than snow and redder than a rose, his hair was all white and like white wool and curly. Glorious was his face. When he opened his eyes, the house shone like the sun. And he stood up from the hands of the midwife, and he opened his mouth and praised the Lord of eternity" (1 Enoch 106:2–3). Lamech, therefore, suspects that the child is not his but that a watcher had fathered the child: "I think he is not from me, but from the angels" (1 Enoch 106:6), only to be reassured by his father, Methuselah, and grandfather, Enoch, that this was not so. In the other version in the Genesis Apocryphon, his wife Bitenosh reminded Lamech of the exhilarating sex they had once had and accounted for the outcome accordingly. Lamech reports, "Then Bitenosh, my wife, spoke to me very harshly, and . . . said: "O my brother and lord! Remember our sexual pleasure . . . in the heat of intercourse, and the gasping of my breath in my breast. . . . I swear to you by the Great Holy One, by the King of the heavens . . . that this seed comes from you, that this pregnancy comes from you, that the planting of [this] fruit comes from you . . . and not from any foreigner nor from any of the watchers or sins of heaven" (1QapGen III, 8–10, 14–16). The first columns of Genesis Apocryphon, whose remains are fragmentary, retold the watcher myth in the words of the watchers themselves, apparently in a form close to what we find in Jubilees, speaking of themselves as having been sent to earth initially by God (1QapGen I, 26–27), but now imprisoned awaiting judgement.

The Book of Biblical Antiquities (abbreviated as LAB), sometime called Pseudo-Philo, written in the mid to late first century CE, retells Israel's history. It, too, includes the story of the wicked watchers. In doing so, it concurs with Jubilees in having the angels described as being initially sent on a commission by God (LAB 34:1–5).

The collection in 1 Enoch contains also a document usually named the Parables of Enoch (1 Enoch 37–71). It is the latest of the various writings drawn together there as works of Enoch and was probably composed as late as the first century CE. In alluding to the myth, it focuses especially on Asael, for whom it uses the alternative name, Azazel. It focuses on his teaching of metallurgy and sorcery and sees it in a negative light. Indeed, it uses Azazel and his fate as a warning especially to kings who will also face fiery judgement if they follow the ways of violence and war.

Around the same time, another writing attributed to Enoch appeared: 2 Enoch. It, too, mentions the angels' fall, as does 2 Baruch. 2 Baruch was written in the late first century CE in the aftermath of the recapture of Jerusalem by the Romans in 70 CE after they crushed the revolt. It uses the watcher myth to warn of the dangers which attractive women pose for angels and men (56:10–11) and also of the dangers of intermarriage with foreigners (56:12). The Apocalypse of Abraham (late first century CE), like 2 Baruch, written in the aftermath of the fall of Jerusalem, mentions the angels' defilement and their leadership of foreign nations.

Some writers were very in touch with the literature and stories of the wider Greek culture. It had been dominant in the eastern Mediterranean and remained influential after the Roman empire was established. This is, in part why Paul and other early leaders in the church wrote in Greek.

Beginning in the mid-second century BCE and continuing until the seventh century CE a series of poetic writings appeared purporting to be oracles, uttered by the legendary Greek priestess, Sibyl. The series is called the Sibylline Oracles. It followed an established trend in the Greco-Roman world. The Jewish and Christian Sibylline Oracles inevitably reflected some influence from the myth. Among its first compositions is what is now called Sibylline Oracles Book 3, composed mid-second century BCE probably in the large Jewish community in Alexandria, Egypt. Like Judith, it makes a connection between the giants and the Hellenistic myth of the Titans, equally fearsome monsters from the past (Sibylline Oracles 3:110–55). Sibylline Oracles books 1–2, written probably mid-first century CE, mentions the watchers, but in very positive terms, reflecting the versions which saw their initial activity as helpful and instructive.

The Wisdom of Solomon, included in the Apocrypha, was written in the early first century CE in the name of King Solomon, who lived a full millennium earlier. It, too, reflects a Greco-Roman setting. It has the giants drown in the great flood (14:6), as in the Animal Apocalypse. The myth is foundational for another writing composed in the name of Solomon, the Testament of Solomon (some of it late-first century CE, some of it later). In it, demons have a voice and claim descent from the watchers (2:4; 5:3; 5:8). They boast of their exploits of seduction, buggery, rape, and corruption of even great king Solomon (8:11). They include both Beelzeboul who claims special status (6:1) and Asmodeus, the demon who in the book of Tobit kills men on their wedding night (8:3; cf. Tobit 3:8).

The Testaments of the Twelve Patriarchs, in its present form given a Christian framework and workover probably in the second century CE, contains much material that is earlier, including about the myth. It has each patriarch, each of Jacob's twelve sons, offer advice to his future descendants. That advice is based in part of on stories told in Genesis. In the Testament of Reuben, Reuben is portrayed as a model of sexual wrongdoing because he raped Bilhah, his father's concubine (Genesis 35:22). Reuben, therefore, warns his descendants against sexual wrongdoing. In doing so, he blames the women as having seduced the watchers (Testament of Reuben 5:6–7), attributing this, as in the myth in 1 Enoch 8, to Asael, who taught people how to make jewelry and cosmetics.

The author of the Testaments somewhat demythologizes the story about the angels and the women by claiming that the angels "changed themselves into the shape of men, and they appeared to them [the women] when they were having sexual intercourse with their husbands" (Testament of Reuben 5:6). Accordingly, "they, lusting in their mind after their appearances, bore giants; for the watchers appeared to them as reaching unto heaven" (5:7). The assumption is that the angels were thereby able to plant their seed into the women's wombs, perhaps analogous to how people might have understood the conception without male involvement of Jesus and Melchizedek, not as an act of sexual intercourse but as a supernatural achievement (Matthew 1:18; Luke 1:31, 35; 2 Enoch 71:30).

In the Testament of Naphtali, the author links Sodom's sin to sexual wrongdoing by declaring that the Sodomites changed the order of their nature and so engaged in sexual relations with other men, sodomy, just as the watchers had acted contrary to their created nature (Testament of Naphtali 3:3–5; 4:1).

The Watcher Myth and the New Testament

The myth, touched on in Genesis 6 and developed in 1 Enoch, was widely known and influential in New Testament times. The author of Jude cites 1 Enoch 1:9, when he writes, "It was also about these that Enoch, in the seventh generation from Adam, prophesied, saying, 'See, the Lord is coming with tens of thousands of his holy ones, ¹⁵to execute judgement on all, and to convict everyone of all the deeds of ungodliness that they have committed in such an ungodly way, and of all the harsh things that ungodly sinners have spoken against him'" (Jude 14–15). Jude mentions "the angels who did not keep their own position, but left their proper dwelling, he has kept in eternal chains in deepest darkness for the judgment of the great day" alongside the sexual sin of Sodom and Gomorrah (Jude 6–7), as does 2 Pet 2:4–10. Paul reflects knowledge of the myth when he argues that women engaged in worship should not abandon their usual head scarves. Why? "Because of the angels" (1 Cor 11:10). Perhaps when 1 Peter portrays Jesus between his death and resurrection as addressing the spirits in prison, he was doing just that: announcing to the imprisoned watchers their defeat (3:19).

More broadly, people understood the reason why things are the way they are by using the myth. Thus, they explained illnesses physical and mental by pointing to evil spirits. This assumption underlines the stories of Jesus' healings and exorcisms.

The earliest accounts of Jesus' ministry depict him as often healing by exorcism. Indeed, he is reported as citing such exorcisms as proofs that God's reign, promised to liberate people from the powers that oppressed them, was breaking in. "But if it is by the finger of God that I cast out the demons, then the kingdom of God has come to you" (Luke 11:20). Matthew and Luke share the same source material at this point, so that the same saying with little variation occurs in Matthew 12:28.

When in the earliest Gospel, Mark, John the Baptist announces that Jesus will baptize with the Spirit (1:8), he is pointing forward to Jesus' healing ministry, which Mark goes on to recount. The first deed of Jesus reported in Mark after he calls his disciples is a healing by exorcism in the synagogue (Mark 1:21–28). Mark portrays as empowered by the Spirit and so enabled to expel demons and bring liberation and healing.

Mark's account of Jesus' defense in 3:22–30 against the charge that he performed exorcisms in league with the chief of demons makes this clear. There Mark has Jesus respond to the charge as follows: "Truly I tell you, people will be forgiven for their sins and whatever blasphemies they utter; but whoever blasphemes against the Holy Spirit can never have forgiveness, but is guilty of an eternal sin" (Mark 3:28–29). Mark explains: "For they had said, 'He has an unclean spirit'" (Mark 3:30) and had earlier reported: "The scribes who came down from Jerusalem said, 'He has Beelzebul, and by the ruler of the demons he casts out demons'" (Mark 3:22). Jesus' ministry was, as John had said, a baptizing of people with the Spirit, bringing them liberation and healing through exorcism.

The myth of the wicked angels whose misdeeds ultimately let loose the unclean spirits to plague humanity provides the framework for understanding human need and Jesus' response to it. Jesus' healings and exorcisms are cited as major evidence that in his ministry God's reign was breaking in, liberating people from the powers that oppressed them. That was their science and their psychology which framed their message of good news.

Making Sense of the Myth Today

The myth of the watchers meets us as a story on the margins of the story of Israel. From around the fourth century BCE onwards we find it receiving increased attention, particularly in those circles which sought explanations for the troubles of humanity. Israel's suffering, being banished into exile by the Babylonians in the early sixth century BCE and then being returned to their land half a century later to something far less than what prophets had promised and hoped for, created a crisis for faith.

Was God no longer in control? Had it really been their own fault? Was it really divine punishment that left them seeing themselves as "the poor"? Job's story helped to press the issue further, the suffering of a good man. Was God somehow making Israel suffer as his servant to take on themselves the judgement which others deserved, as the author of Isa 53 suggested? For some, the solution lay in hoping not for immediate divine intervention in the short term to save them but in envisaging a new beginning for them and for all creation, indeed a new heaven and a new earth: "I am about to create new heavens and a new earth; the former things shall not be remembered or come to mind. . . . The wolf and the lamb shall feed together, the lion shall eat straw like the ox; but the serpent—its food shall be dust! They shall not hurt or destroy on all my holy mountain, says the LORD" (Isaiah 65:17, 25). Imagination flowed and poetry flourished with images of prosperity and abundance, including for some a generous welcoming of peoples of other nations to have a place around God's temple, their swords made into ploughs and their spears into pruning hooks:

> In days to come the mountain of the LORD's house shall be established as the highest of the mountains, and shall be raised above the hills; all the nations shall stream to it. . . . ⁴He shall judge between the nations, and shall arbitrate for many peoples; they shall beat their swords into ploughshares, and their spears into

pruning-hooks; nation shall not lift up sword against nation, neither shall they learn war any more. (Isaiah 2:2, 4)

There must be a setting right, a day of judgement, and for that, hope moved
to envisage a raising back to life of the righteous or even of all peoples so
that they could be brought to justice.

For many, the explanations that Israel's and humanity's current plight
was their own fault, from Adam and Eve's sin onward, no longer sufficed.
There was more going on which needed to be accounted for. The invad-
ing nations were surely no better than Israel and deserved punishment
just as much. The myth of the watchers offered an explanation. Things
went badly wrong when some angels committed their great sin and so let
disaster loose on humankind.

What may once have been an innocent explanation of the origin of
giants of which many cultures had stories, namely heavenly beings impreg-
nating human women, became a paradigm of things going wrong, contrary
to nature, contrary to God's order. Perhaps informed by the often disastrous
consequences of sexual wrongdoing in human households and communities, the storytellers depicted these angels as crossing forbidden boundaries
and so setting disaster in motion.

Yes, the outcome was giants, but these were no gentle giants of culture's fairy tales. They were monsters creating havoc such as some had
experienced amid scenes of war and carnage. Whether in the form of
seeing evil spirits emerge from their cadavers or seeing them as directly
generated by the angels themselves, the outcome of the watchers' flagrant
transgression of God's order out of sexual lust set dangerous forces loose
in the world. They were to plague humanity with physical and mental illnesses, and worse, to seduce humanity into idolatry and to exert corrupt
control over nations. This was a better explanation than that suffering was
all somebody's fault. It was, indeed, a more scientific explanation to say that
such forces, which we do not personalize in the same way, roam our reality
and confront us with challenges to survive.

Future hope had, therefore, to mean finally bringing these spirits,
these demons, into submission, so that, alongside bringing humans to account, these demons and their leaders, called by their various titles, Satan,
Beelzebul, Mastema, Lucifer, must finally be bound and destroyed.

From a myth on the margins to a central explanation of reality, the story
of human plight, depicted in the myth, informed people's understanding of
human need and so also of the importance of Jesus' ministry. He announced

God's reign and cited his expulsion of demons and acts of healing, also undoing the demon's deeds, as evidence of hope: God's victory was at hand. His followers saw in the defeat of his death not a failure, a victory for the demons, but a climax, paradoxically a victory of God's Spirit, love, sealed in their assertion of his resurrection. They read from it the promise that he would be God's agent, for which they used other images, including those considered in the chapters which follow in this book, and that in his name already in the interim people could be liberated from the powers that oppressed them. This was about sin, but it was always about more than that and, as Paul expounds it, sin itself is a power to be exorcized by the Spirit.

In the world of today, our explanations for the state of humanity both differ and echo the myth of old. We do not personalize the viruses which circulate in our own time, whether the dramatic COVID virus or any other, but we share with the mythmakers the understanding that illnesses are not engendered by God as punishment or testing but exist out there in reality. We will explain their origin differently, not by myth, but by evolution and adaptation. We will share the goal of seeking to set people free from the debilitating effects of illness, physical or mental. We will stand in continuity with Jesus in seeking to promote health and healing, even if our medical practices are far from the first-century means and methods he shared with his contemporaries.

Their science is not our science. Our world is not flat or a sphere around which the sun circles. Our explanations of physical and mental illness are very different. This means that if we are to take anything from the stories of Jesus, they are that it is God's will that we seek to liberate people from the powers that oppress them. For us that means healing of mental and physical illness. The intent and mission remain the same: compassion and healing, even if our explanations differ in major ways. We have to translate such stories of Jesus into our own world and our own terms, but love, the fruit of the Spirit which generated those initiatives then, remains our inspiration.

We will also not embrace theories of nations being under the control of demons, but we will recognize what those theories sought to address, namely that governments do sometimes exercise violence and that systems do inhibit and sometimes crush life and hope. Health and healing have to be bigger than helping individuals. We need to recognize the larger dynamics and systems which hold people in poverty and oppress their freedom. They recognized that in their way in the framework of their demonology. We need to recognize it, too. Our world now adds new dimensions of need they did not see, not least the danger to the planet's well-being from increased carbon emission and human induced climate change.

We recognize the reality they sought to address with their watcher myth. It is our reality. We can learn from their response even as we translate it into our current understandings of reality and in the process subject it to scrutiny. We reject, for instance, the assumptions about women's sexuality as dangerous, as reflected in some versions of the myth, and the assumption in one version that sexual intercourse is acceptable only when people engage in it for the purpose of reproducing the species.

Nevertheless, despite these differences and the distance between their science and ours, we respect that this was how these Jews, including Jesus and his followers, sought to account for the plight of humans. In their wisdom they did so in ways that went far beyond individual guilt and accountability and set before us, therefore, a vision of liberation which was wide and comprehensive alongside a faith that there would be hope, a hope that ultimately believed in love. We can embrace that vision and love and let it find articulation in ways that make sense in our day.

3

The Myth of Divine Kingship

A THRONE, A CROWN, a scepter, courtiers bowing or kneeling, a king in resplendent attire: these are images of the ancient royal courts. Some suggest that it was above all through Alexander the Great and his conquests in the east in the fourth century BCE, reaching as far as India, that such fashions found their way into his world and the west or was it already well underway? By the time of the Roman emperors the pattern had taken hold, some of them indeed claiming to be gods. This was no innovation. Pharaohs of Egypt had claimed the same, millennia before, and rulers of Mesopotamia did similarly. It was never an exact art, but the claims of divine connection, whether by adoption or creation, were sustained despite such gods being often exposed as all too human.

If you were a peasant struggling for survival, it perhaps made sense. The despot who ruled you was like a god, controlling your life. If you were the peasant's lord, it made good sense because it matched your own ambition to have power, influence and control. Second best, you can be the king's liege, his courtier and supporter, lead his army or gather his taxes.

Ask, who was the greatest among humankind and the answer was plain for all to see: the king. The royal court rituals of deference, the pageantry, the wealth, and the splendor said it all. Great is our king. God save the king!

God as King and Kings as Gods

It should not surprise us that religious leaders seized on such images to depict God's greatness. It was not that images of God's heavenly court inspired the rituals of deference to the human sovereign. The other way round! Human images inspired images of God. God is king, seated on a throne, surrounded by angels, his courtiers, who forever bow and kneel before him, in splendor unimaginable. Of course, there was two-way traffic. The earthly image inspired the heavenly and the heavenly inspired the earthly. Sometimes people made it sound as though prayer was like pleading with a self-preoccupied monarch to give some attention to people in need, as though God needs prompting to observe and to care, just like the self-indulgent despots whose chief interests were their own power and glory. Such models corrupt worship and so perpetuate corrupt values which usurp love.

The high echelons of humanity were not easily satisfied just with control and subjugation. Many saw themselves as belonging to the divine, themselves gods in the pantheon that determined human affairs. And long after such models of human governance have lost their respect and validity, the model of God they inspired still persists. Royal court rituals still shape many liturgies and their forms of expression, from acts of obeisance to language. Just look at our hymn books! Monarchs were usually male and so male images populate common piety to this day.

I can remember as a schoolboy learning history, which in New Zealand of those days had to include much of British history. That British history introduced me to the notion of the divine right of kings, claims which persisted at least into the seventeenth century. My study of Classics introduced me to emperor worship and this, in turn, made connections for me not only with the persecutions in Christian beginnings, but also with the earlier version of divine kingship which came to characterize Israel. This is where we will begin.

The Myth of Divine Kingship in Israel

The myth of divine kingship in Israel was that God adopted or at least enlisted the king as his Son at his coronation. Thus Psalm 2 has a king declare: "I will tell of the decree of the LORD: He said to me, 'You are my son; today I have begotten you. [8]Ask of me, and I will make the nations your heritage, and the ends of the earth your possession. [9]You shall break them with a rod of iron, and dash them in pieces like a potter's vessel'" (Psalm 2:7–9). In Psalm 110 a courtier declares: "The LORD says to my lord, 'Sit at my right hand until I make your enemies your footstool'" (Psalm 110:1). Psalm 89 has God declare of David: "He shall cry to me, 'You are my Father, my God, and the Rock of my salvation!' [27]I will make him the firstborn, the highest of the kings of the earth" (Psalm 89:26–27). The assumption is that other kings are also divine sons, but this promised one will be their superior, as a firstborn son was held to be superior to his siblings. The prophet Nathan is reported as declaring God's promise to David's son, Solomon, which will have inspired that psalm: "When your days are fulfilled and you lie down with your ancestors, I will raise up your offspring after you, who shall come forth from your body, and I will establish his kingdom. ^{13}He shall build a house for my name, and I will establish the throne of his kingdom for ever. ^{14}I will be a father to him, and he shall be a son to me" (2 Samuel 7:12–14). There was a level of restraint in Israel which kept them from declaring the king a god, although to be God's adopted vice-regent on earth and so his son did sometimes lead to the king being addressed as "God." We see this in Psalm 45: "Your throne, O God, endures for ever and ever. Your royal scepter is a scepter of equity; ^{7}you love righteousness and hate wickedness. Therefore God, your God, has anointed you with the oil of gladness beyond your companions; ^{8}your robes are all fragrant with myrrh and aloes and cassia. From ivory palaces stringed instruments make you glad; ^{9}daughters of kings are among your ladies of honor; at your right hand stands the queen in gold of Ophir" (Psalm 45:6–9). We may speculate about when and how such notions of divine kingship entered Israel's heritage. Psalm 110, cited above, may offer a clue. For, having reported the king's enthronement as lord at God's right hand, in its fourth verse it declares of the king: "The LORD has sworn and will not change his mind, 'You are a priest for ever according to the order of Melchizedek'" (Psalm 110:4).

In ancient court cultures, kings were the people's spokespersons before God, thus exercising a priestly role, so it should not surprise us to see the king declared to be also a priest. There are two elements in this text which are surprising. First, Israel had a cult and a hereditary priesthood traced to Aaron, Moses' brother, and further back to Levi, Jacob's son. It was independent of the royal line, for David and his successors were not of the tribe of Levi, but the tribe of Judah.

The second surprising element is also a clue to understanding this anomaly. Genesis 14 tells is that Melchizedek was king and priest in Salem, Jerusalem. David conquered Salem, the Jebusite city, around 1000 BCE and, it appears likely, adopted its royal rituals. Accordingly, he and his successors became priests of the order of Melchizedek. Later when people wanted to talk of Jesus as a priest, who was also not a descendant of Levi and Aaron, they seized on this anomaly and declared Jesus, too, a priest of the order of Melchizedek (Hebrews 7:11–14), although he was of the tribe of Judah, not Levi.

Israel's adaptation of the myth of divine kingship was not without controversy and the behavior of subsequent kings did not exactly help, including David's atrocious behavior of having the husband of Bathsheba (whom David abducted from her household) killed (2 Samuel 11), not to speak of Solomon and his harem.

The books of Samuel bring us traditions with rough edges, often not smoothed out through the editorial processes. Samuel was Israel's de facto leader and stood in succession to a series of charismatic, mainly military leaders, called "judges," during the early days of settlement of the mixed tribes as they moved into Canaan. The book of Judges tells their stories. Famously, Samuel was very reluctant to agree to the appointment of a king in Israel. The report in 1 Samuel has him declare:

> These will be the ways of the king who will reign over you: he will take your sons and appoint them to his chariots and to be his horsemen, and to run before his chariots; [12]and he will appoint for himself commanders of thousands and commanders of fifties, and some to plough his ground and to reap his harvest, and to make his implements of war and the equipment of his chariots. [13]He will take your daughters to be perfumers and cooks and bakers. [14]He will take the best of your fields and vineyards and olive orchards and give them to his courtiers. [15]He will take one-tenth of your grain and of your vineyards and give it to his officers and his courtiers. [16]He will take your male and female slaves, and the best of your cattle and donkeys, and put them to his work. [17]He will take one-tenth of your flocks, and you shall be his slaves. [18]And in that day you will cry out because of your king, whom you have chosen for yourselves; but the LORD will not answer you in that day. (1 Samuel 8:11–18)

The story continues with God's suggesting that Samuel go along, however reluctantly, with the people's request for a king, which then leads to the anointing of Saul and subsequently, after his failure and demise, the anointing of David, a young shepherd, from Bethlehem. Thus began the Davidic dynasty. The stories of Samuel are not flattering about kingship. Granting one person absolute power was as doubtful then as it is now. There were kings hailed as good and some hailed as bad. The editors who composed the histories preserved in the books of Samuel and Kings and who reflect the critical values enshrined in the book of Deuteronomy make that clear. Kings ought to act justly and care about their citizens. Most did not. Much earlier in ancient Egypt, the image of an ideal king was one who not only controlled but also cared for his people as a shepherd did for his sheep.

Though not gods, kings claimed to be God's representative on earth, adopted into God's ruling family as his sons. It was hard to gainsay such claims, let along depose kings. A prime minister of Australia of strongly charismatic Christian bent once, it seems naively, declared that God had called him to be prime minister. The absurd inappropriateness of such a claim if taken literally, which meant one should vote for him, was obvious to most but illustrates the dangers which such claims posed. It took centuries for nations to puncture the pretensions of such royal ideology and those still with its vestiges have largely reduced it to symbolic representation, somewhat helped by female incumbency on the British throne. The future of such anomalous vestiges embedded in a persistent class system is uncertain.

Hope for Peace and Justice at the Hands of a King Like David

The failure of all but a few monarchs of the Davidic dynasty in the north as Israel and the south as Judah was a malaise frequently confronted by Israel's prophets. The gap between the ideals and hopes of the Davidic line and reality was painfully vast. The king's role was to keep the people safe from its enemies and to ensure justice in the land. They could do little in relation to the former in the face of mighty empires and in relation to the latter they were mostly deemed to have failed.

The northern kingdom, Israel, came to an end in the late eighth century at the hands of the Assyrian empire. The southern kingdom, Judah, came to an end in the early sixth century, at the hands of the Babylonian empire when most of its inhabitants were deported to Babylonia, present-day Iraq. It was there that hopes began to arise both for a return to Judah and Jerusalem and also for the reestablishment of the Davidic dynasty. Some longed for such an anointed king.

The Hebrew word for "anointed" is *mashiach*, transliterated popularly into English as Messiah. Those who could entertain positive images of kingship and who saw it as God's preferred option gave expression to the hope that such a Son of David, an anointed king, God's vice regent and adopted Son, would arise and restore the nation's fortunes. In time, the reference to such a figure as the Anointed One, in Hebrew "the Messiah," morphed

from being a description to being a title. In the New Testament, we sometimes find the Hebrew word, Messiah, left untranslated. Sometimes we find
it translated. In Greek, Anointed One is *Christos*, which comes through as
the Christ in English. That, too, soon morphed into a title and even became
more like a name: Christ, easily misunderstood as such.

Christians tend to imagine that the major focus of hope was the person, the agent, the Messiah, matching the centrality of the person of Jesus
in Christian faith. This, however, slightly distorts the emphasis of Jewish
tradition, where the primary basis of hope was God and God's action, not
so much the agents whom God might use for such action, who might be
an angel, a prophet, a priest, or a king as leader. This is why they could
entertain various options, including various agents as leaders, for how God
would change things for the better.

The book of Isaiah contains a hope for the birth of such a leader:

> For a child has been born for us, a son given to us; authority rests
> upon his shoulders; and he is named Wonderful Counsellor,
> Mighty God, Everlasting Father, Prince of Peace. [7]His authority
> shall grow continually, and there shall be endless peace for the
> throne of David and his kingdom. He will establish and uphold
> it with justice and with righteousness from this time onwards and
> for evermore. (Isaiah 9:6–7)

Israel's version of the divine kingship myth is clearly visible in this oracle,
especially in the names where he is declared to be "Mighty God," not in the
sense of being a second God, but as God's representative, reflecting the daring use of language noted above in Psalm 45. The traditional expectation of
the king's dual role as bringing justice and righteousness among the people
and protecting them from their enemies is clearly present, especially in the
words which come immediately before this passage: "For the yoke of their
burden, and the bar across their shoulders, the rod of their oppressor, you
have broken as on the day of Midian. [5]For all the boots of the tramping
warriors and all the garments rolled in blood shall be burned as fuel for
the fire" (Isaiah 9:4–5). Key elements of the anointed king's role are thus to
overcome enemies and establish peace and justice. This is very apparent also
in Isaiah 11, which speaks of the hope for a Davidic king (similarly 16:4–5).
"A shoot shall come out from the stock of Jesse, and a branch shall grow out
of his roots. [2]The spirit of the LORD shall rest on him, the spirit of wisdom
and understanding, the spirit of counsel and might, the spirit of knowledge
and the fear of the LORD" (Isaiah 11:1–2). It gives particular emphasis to

peace and justice, especially for the poor: "He shall not judge by what his eyes see, or decide by what his ears hear; ⁴but with righteousness he shall judge the poor, and decide with equity for the meek of the earth; he shall strike the earth with the rod of his mouth, and with the breath of his lips he shall kill the wicked" (Isaiah 11:3–4). His role will have universal significance, resulting in the return of exiles. "On that day the root of Jesse shall stand as a signal to the peoples; the nations shall inquire of him, and his dwelling shall be glorious. ¹¹On that day the Lord will extend his hand yet a second time to recover the remnant that is left of his people, from Assyria, from Egypt, from Pathros, from Ethiopia, from Elam, from Shinar, from Hamath, and from the coastlands of the sea. ¹²He will raise a signal for the nations, and will assemble the outcasts of Israel, and gather the dispersed of Judah from the four corners of the earth" (Isaiah 11:10–12).

The book of Isaiah is at base a collection of prophetic oracles spoken by the prophet, Isaiah, in the northern kingdom of Israel, shortly before it was overrun by the Assyrians, in the late eighth century BCE. Over the following centuries oracles by other prophets were added. One major block runs from chapter 40 to 55 and another from chapter 56 to 66, both from the mid to late sixth century. In addition, other passages came into the collection as supplements and updating. Such is this text just cited. It clearly reflects the post-exilic world, probably emanating from the fifth century BCE at the earliest, some three centuries after the original Isaiah was active.

The hope, which grew in intensity over time the more hopeless situations became, rests in part on belief that God had made a covenant, a promise, that David's dynasty would have a future, a belief that its survival was guaranteed. Those parts of Isaiah emanating from the Babylonian exile in the sixth century reflect this hope that Israel would be restored and God would renew that covenant, raise up a leader and commander, and give Israel a central place among the nations: "Incline your ear, and come to me; listen, so that you may live. I will make with you an everlasting covenant, my steadfast, sure love for David. ⁴See, I made him a witness to the peoples, a leader and commander for the peoples. ⁵See, you shall call nations that you do not know, and nations that do not know you shall run to you, because of the LORD your God, the Holy One of Israel, for he has glorified you" (Isaiah 55:3–5).

The prophet Jeremiah, active in the early sixth century BCE, clearly makes such hope conditional on the Davidic kings ruling with justice and compassion. He addresses Judah's last ruler accordingly: "To the house of the king of Judah say: Hear the word of the LORD, [12]O house of David! Thus says the LORD: Execute justice in the morning, and deliver from the hand of the oppressor anyone who has been robbed, or else my wrath will go forth like fire, and burn, with no one to quench it, because of your evil doings" (Jeremiah 21:11–12; similarly, 22:1–5). In a similar vein, Jeremiah has God declare woes against the shepherds (rulers) of Israel, but holds out hope for something better: "The days are surely coming, says the LORD, when I will raise up for David a righteous Branch, and he shall reign as king and deal wisely, and shall execute justice and righteousness in the land. [6]In his days Judah will be saved and Israel will live in safety. And this is the name by which he will be called: 'The LORD is our righteousness'" (Jeremiah 23:5; 33:15–16; similarly, 30:8).

Later generations expanded upon these hopes, incorporating the following into the book of Jeremiah which its earlier version preserved in the Greek translation did not yet include:

> For thus says the LORD: David shall never lack a man to sit on the throne of the house of Israel, [18]and the levitical priests shall never lack a man in my presence to offer burnt-offerings, to make grain-offerings, and to make sacrifices for all time. [19]The word of the LORD came to Jeremiah: [20]Thus says the LORD: If any of you could break my covenant with the day and my covenant with the night, so that day and night would not come at their appointed time, [21]only then could my covenant with my servant David be broken, so that he would not have a son to reign on his throne, and my covenant with my ministers the Levites. [22]Just as the host of heaven cannot be numbered and the sands of the sea cannot be measured, so I will increase the offspring of my servant David, and the Levites who minister to me. (Jeremiah 33:17–22)

Like Jeremiah, Ezekiel (early sixth century BCE) has God warn the shepherds of Israel who abuse and exploit the flock given to them, and promise that a king in David's line would come to the rescue: "I will set up over them one shepherd, my servant David, and he shall feed them: he shall feed them and be their shepherd. [24]And I, the LORD, will be their God, and my servant David shall be prince among them; I, the LORD, have spoken" (Ezekiel 34:23–24; similarly 37:24–25).

At one of their low points, experiencing exile from their homeland, some dreamt in glowing terms of a return to Zion, sometimes with no reference to reestablishment of the Davidic monarchy. Such dreams are reflected in one of the major supplements to the book of Isaiah mentioned above. Indeed, the prophet whose writings were incorporated in Isa 40–55 even depicts Cyrus the Persian as God's anointed, at least as his agent in enabling the people to return from exile in the late sixth century. The Medes and Persians conquered the Babylonians and under Cyrus released the exiled Israelites to return to their land. Those who did return, however, could form only a small city-state in subjection to the Persians, led by a governor, Zerubbabel, and a high priest, Joshua. Under their leadership the temple was rebuilt and dedicated in 516 BCE, but it was far from its former glory and the dreams of a paradisal return vanished into a struggle for survival.

Haggai, a prophet active in the days after the return, claimed to hear God's declaration of liberation through Zerubbabel:

> Speak to Zerubbabel, governor of Judah, saying, I am about to shake the heavens and the earth, [22]and to overthrow the throne of kingdoms; I am about to destroy the strength of the kingdoms of the nations, and overthrow the chariots and their riders; and the horses and their riders shall fall, every one by the sword of a comrade. [23]On that day, says the LORD of hosts, I will take you, O Zerubbabel my servant, son of Shealtiel, says the LORD, and make you like a signet ring; for I have chosen you, says the LORD of hosts. (Haggai 2:21–23)

It did not happen. The prophet, Zechariah, whose visions and oracles are found in Zechariah 1–8, wrote at the about the same time as Haggai. He, too, mentions Joshua and Zerubbabel. In one passage he spoke of the crowning of Zerubbabel, although the text was subsequently altered to read "Joshua," resulting in confusion because it created two priestly figures. The confusion will have led ancient translations altering the text to read "crowns" instead of "crown." The text spoke originally of creating a single crown, to crown Zerubbabel king, who would rule alongside Joshua the high priest. The version which has survived has the high priest, Joshua, crowned instead:

> Take the silver and gold and make a crown, and set it on the head of the high priest Joshua son of Jehozadak; [12]say to him: Thus says the LORD of hosts: Here is a man whose name is Branch: for he shall branch out in his place, and he shall build the temple of the LORD. [13]It is he that shall build the temple of the LORD; he shall bear royal honor, and shall sit and rule on his throne. There shall be a priest by his throne, with peaceful understanding between the two of them. (Zechariah 6:11–13)

The changes may indeed reflect the fact that the role of the secular leaders, Zerubbabel and his successors, diminished beside that of the high priest as the nation took the shape of being a temple state.

There was also now much more to hope for than a dynasty. There were people still in exile and scattered abroad. There was the Persian empire in control. Hope increasingly focused on bringing the people home and also of bringing the nations into submission or at least bringing them to respect Israel's people and live with them in admiration and peace. As already in the oracles of what is frequently called Second Isaiah, namely Isaiah 40–55, so also in 56–66, the focus is no longer on the agents, such as hope for a king, but on the need for a changed state of affairs, for restoration, justice and peace.

The prophet whose works were added to Zechariah's as chapters 9–14 has God point to Israel's liberation from oppression from the surrounding nations. It still sees this in terms of the restoration of the glory of the Davidic house. It also still reflects adapted elements of the divine kingship myth: the house of David will be like God and the angel of the Lord. "On that day the LORD will shield the inhabitants of Jerusalem, so that the feeblest among them on that day shall be like David, and the house of David shall be like God, like the angel of the LORD, at their head. ⁹And on that day I will seek to destroy all the nations that come against Jerusalem" (Zechariah 12:8–9). The prophet's realism about the fallibility of the Davidic dynasty therefore includes forgiveness and cleansing in the image of hope: "On that day a fountain shall be opened for the house of David and the inhabitants of Jerusalem, to cleanse them from sin and impurity" (Zechariah 13:1). The belief in God's guarantee of the Davidic dynasty persisted within the broader context of hope for renewal. Ben Sira, now in the Apocrypha, writing in the early second century BCE, links hope for the future of David's dynasty with a similar guarantee of the heritage of Aaron's priesthood (Ben Sira 45:25). It is like the passage from Jeremiah 33 cited above. He declares that God "will never blot out the descendants of his chosen one, or destroy the family line of him who loved him. So he gave a remnant to Jacob, and to David a root from his own family" (Ben Sira 47:22). He asserts this hope despite the failures of the kings of whom he writes: "Except for David and Hezekiah and Josiah, all of them were great sinners, for they abandoned the law of the Most High; the kings of Judah came to an end" (Ben Sira 49:4).

Hope for an Anointed King Like David but Much More

From the end of the sixth century onwards, increasingly, hope also morphed from restoration and renewal in the city-state to visions of God intervening to restart creation. Born of hopeless experience and hopeful faith, prophets arose who saw little change emerging in the future without a major reset of the world's powers and systems. Sometimes such visions had little or no place for a renewed Davidic kingship. A new creation was needed and that meant going beyond the idealization of David's reign to notions of a return to paradise.

Already the prophet responsible for Isaiah 56–66 spoke of hope in these terms, portraying God as grounding hope in macro-change: "For I am about to create new heavens and a new earth; the former things shall not be remembered or come to mind. [18]But be glad and rejoice for ever in what I am creating; for I am about to create Jerusalem as a joy, and its people as a delight" (Isaiah 65:17–18). For some, Davidic kingship remained a current hope, at least as a preparation for that ultimate solution, but it would take more than a Davidic king to set things right. There needed to be intervention from on high.

We find these hopes also expressed in several of the Jewish writings found from 1947 onwards in the caves by the Dead Sea, called the Dead Sea Scrolls, which we met in the last chapter in discussing the watcher myth. Some of them focus on hope for a royal Messiah. One of them which also looked to more than just a Davidic king is the so-called War Scroll (1Q33/1QM; on the abbreviations see under "More retellings" in the previous chapter). In it we find, beside the hope for leadership from God's prince, God's Messiah, also the belief that angels would descend from on high to help in battle.

Echoing what the prophet Zechariah dreamt of about what might have been, other authors saw hope in the raising up of a dual leadership, a royal Messiah and a priestly one, the Messiahs of Aaron and Israel, usually with the balance of power favoring the former (1Q28a/Sa II, 11–22). Sometimes they are accompanied by a prophet like Moses (1Q28/1QS IX, 11), or sometimes they are combined into a single figure with both priestly and royal roles (CD XIX, 10–11). The inconsistency and variability in such hopes was not a problem because the focus was ultimately on what God would do, rather than how God would do it and what agents God would employ for the purpose. Among the scrolls there were collections of biblical texts used to support all three figures, the royal and priestly Messiahs and the prophet like Moses (e.g., 4Q174/4QFlor I, 10–13, citing parts of 2 Samuel 7:12–14; 4Q175/4QTestimonia, 9–13, citing Num 24:17).

Such texts of hope emerged from the turbulence which followed the establishment of the Hasmonean dynasty after the success of the Maccabean revolt against the Hellenistic Syrian kingdom of the Seleucids in 167–164 BCE. Led by Judas Maccabeus of the priestly house of Hasmon, the Jews overthrow their Hellenistic Syrian overlords, but what followed as Judas, then his brother, Simon and their descendants ruled, eventually calling themselves kings, was far from satisfactory. Dissatisfaction with both secular and priestly rule produced a revival of hopes for royal and priestly Messiahs.

One document, 4Q521/4QMessianic Apocalypse, attributed a range of benefits that would come through a royal Messiah. "[For the hea]vens and the earth shall listen to His Messiah 2. [and all w]hich is in them shall not turn away from the commandments of the holy ones" (frag. 2 II, 1–2). The words/letters in brackets are added where they are missing in the fragment but are clearly to be assumed. This passage attributes a teaching role to the Messiah. It continues, speaking of God: "For he will honor the pious upon the th[ro]ne of his eternal kingdom, 8.'setting prisoners free, opening the eyes of the blind, raising up those who are bo[wed down' (Ps 146:7–8)" (frag. 2 II, 7–8). This appears to indicate that God will do this through the Messiah. It continues in line 11: "and the Lord shall do glorious things which have not been done, just as he s[aid.] 12. For He shall heal the critically wounded, he shall revive the dead, "he shall send good news to the afflicted" (Isa 61:1). 13. He shall sati[sfy] the [poo]r, he shall lead the uprooted, and the hungry he shall enrich (?)" (4Q521/4QMessianic Apocalypse frag. 2 II, 11–13). Such were the hopes which people later saw as fulfilled in Jesus and his message of good news for the poor.

Authors read prophetic writings as referring to their own time. Thus, they applied promises of a king like David to their own times and saw in them the promise that God would raise up for them a warrior leader to defeat the Romans. They read Isaiah 11:1–5, cited above, as promising that God would raise up a shoot from the stump of Jesse in their time (4Q162/4QIsab 11–25).

Others looked to heavenly intervention by the archangel Michael or by Melchizedek reconceived as of angelic nature (11Q13/11QMelch). The book of Daniel, written during the Maccabean revolt, so, shortly before these writings, presents a vision of God putting Israel back in control. It depicts the nations as like threatening animals and then describes a heavenly figure in the form of a man, "one like a son of man." God gives him control (Daniel 7:13–14). That vision inspired hopes that one day that vision would become reality. The "one like a son of man," sometimes described as the Son of Man, would one day come, often seen as an individual figure. Inevitably that figure acquired royal messianic traits, as in the Parables of Enoch (first century CE). It depicts the Son of Man as God's Messiah, God's Chosen One, and as the one not only to defeat Israel's enemies but also to bring them to judgement (1 Enoch 46; 48; 61–62).

Another document, written as an exposition of Daniel, 4Q246/ 4QapocrDan ar, refers to a figure of whom it writes: "He will be called the Son of God, they will call him the son of the Most High" (II, 1), almost certainly an allusion to a royal messianic figure and probably associated with the figure of the Son of Man in Daniel 7 whose motifs it reflects. It speaks of the people being oppressed until they rise up (presumably under this figure as leader): "Then all will have rest from warfare. 5. Their kingdom will be an eternal kingdom, and all their paths will be righteous. They will judge 6. the land justly, and all (nations) will make peace. Warfare will cease from the land, 7. and all the nations shall do homage to them. The great God will be their help, 8. He Himself will fight for them, putting peoples into their power, all of them 9. he will overthrow before them. God's rule will be an eternal rule" (4Q246/4QapocrDan ar II, 4–9).

God would act through agents, but the primary basis of hope was God, himself, as they saw it, God's action, God re-establishing his reign, the reign or kingdom of God. There was some tolerance for diversity in depicting which agents God would use. A Davidic king Messiah was very common in such hopes. Ousting the Romans was uppermost with those seeking to turn hope into reality.

Another important writing for tracing hopes for a royal Messiah is the Psalms of Solomon. It is a collection of psalms attributed by their editor to King Solomon but composed mid- to late first century BCE. They bemoan Israel's plight at the hand of foreign powers (the Romans) and at one point exclaim: "See, Lord, and raise up for them their king, the son of David to rule over your servant Israel in the time known to you, O God. Undergird him with strength to destroy the unrighteous rulers, to purge Jerusalem from Gentiles" (Psalms of Solomon 7:21–22). It goes on to speak of destroying the unlawful nations, gathering a holy people, and having their king rule over them with wisdom and righteousness. "He will be a righteous king over them, taught by God. There will be no unrighteousness among them in his days, for all shall be holy, and their king shall be the Lord Messiah" (17:32). He will shepherd them as a flock (17:40).

These are all writings before the time of Jesus. Hopes for a royal Messiah continued, however, well after his time. In the late first century CE, 2 Baruch envisages the appearance of the Messiah to rule during an interim time of prosperity and abundance to ensure the hungry are fed before the day of resurrection (2 Baruch 29–30). It speaks of the Messiah destroying enemies and convicting their leaders (2 Baruch 39–40, 70). We find a similar expression of hope in 4 Ezra, now incorporated into 2 Esdras, one of the books of the Apocrypha. It describes the Messiah as like a lion who would overcome Israel's enemies (2 Esdras 12:31–34).

Both authors envisage a two-stage climax to history. Stage one is when the Royal Messiah rules, overcoming Israel's enemies and bringing peace and prosperity, and stage two begins with the resurrection and judgement and eternal bliss or torment. The righteous would then be transformed to become like angels. The same pattern is followed in the book of Revelation, which foresees a thousand-year reign of Jesus as the Messiah on earth, although already accompanied by the resurrected righteous, followed by universal resurrection and judgement day, the punishment of the wicked and blessing of the righteous in a renewed paradise (Revelation 20–22).

The historian Josephus wrote in the second half of the first century CE. He tells the story of what eventually led to the disaster of the destruction of the temple in 70 CE by the Romans. He, himself, had been directly engaged as a commander in Galilee when the revolt against the Romans began in 66 CE. His account of developments lists a range of figures who led movements against Rome's rule. Some had a prophetic profile. A number made the outback desert areas their starting point, highly symbolic in recalling the days before the invasion of Canaan. Some led bands of guerrilla fighters who would harass military forces in raids and retreat to safety. Some leaders styled themselves as God's anointed Messiah.

The second century saw a second major revolt in 132–35 CE, led by Simon ben Kosebah who styled himself Bar Kochba ("Son of the Star"), in allusion to Numbers 24:17, which spoke of a star arising in Israel and a scepter in Jacob. Such imagery also explains the role of the star in Matthew's account of Jesus' birth, a sign of what Matthew is eager to portray, that Jesus is the Messiah.

There were, therefore, various ways of expressing the hope that God would intervene to change things. Among them was the hope for a royal Messiah, an Anointed One, also called the son of David and son of God and in Greek, the Christ. These hopes were alive at the time of Jesus.

Jesus Messiah?

If we ask where Jesus fits into these movements of hope, we find he belongs not with the militants but with the prophetic voices which called for repentance and stricter observance of God's law in the hope that this might prompt divine intervention. These voices included the Pharisees, some of whom merged such devotion with the religious zeal also to fight. As a whole, however, they did not join the major revolt in 66 CE. In their view, one day God would raise up a Messiah. Similarly, the movement with its base at Qumran by the Dead Sea but with enclaves scattered across towns, the Essenes, focused on strict observance of the law. Some of them may also have joined the fight, but primarily they awaited God's intervention. They envisaged final battles with angelic help, such as we noted in the War Scroll referred to above. Fortunately, they protected their library in nearby caves when overrun by the Romans in 69 CE, a rich treasure of scrolls discovered mid last century.

Closest to Jesus of Nazareth among all such movements is John, nicknamed the Baptizer (or Baptist) because he departed from the usual rite of self-immersion and instead called people to let him immerse them as a sign of their submission in repentance to God's will and commitment to obey, and then not in a ritual bath but in the Jordan River. His expectations, sketchily preserved, spoke not of a Davidic king but of God or God's agent about to appear in judgement, wielding an axe or a winnowing fork (Matthew 3:10–12; Luke 3:9, 17). Of Jesus we know much more, not only that he submitted himself to John's baptism, so basically shared his approach, but also that he styled himself not as an ascetic prophet like John, keeping to the desert and limiting his diet and his attire, but instead went into populated areas of Galilee and Judea and ate and drank freely like his fellow citizens.

Our earliest evidence for Jesus among the Gospels comes in the Gospel according to Mark and the sources traceable in Matthew and Luke, one of which they shared, commonly designated "Q," a collection mainly of sayings. This early evidence preserved in these sources of sayings of Jesus and the anecdotes of his interaction with his critics shows that the myth of divine kingship, indeed the issues of Davidic messiahship re-mained, if anywhere, at the margins.

At the center of his message was the reign of God, the kingdom of God, which he announced as impending (Mark 1:14–15). He shared this expecta-tion with John the Baptist, who would have for some time been his mentor. In lifestyle and emphasis, however, he differed from John, especially in his claim that what John saw as future, he saw as already beginning to happen. The reign of God, the kingdom of God, was already beginning to break in. He cited as evidence of this claim the fact that through healing and exorcism the Spirit enabled him to bring liberation to people, thus bringing the reign of God to them already in the present. "If it is by the Spirit of God that I cast out demons, then the kingdom of God has come to you" (Matthew 12:28; similarly, Luke 11:20). As we saw in the previous chapter, the assumption behind accounts of his ministry is that the enemy is primarily to be seen as the swarm of demonic forces which plague humanity.

Nothing in this early evidence suggests that he set out to claim to be the Davidic Messiah. This is so striking that some have speculated that it must nevertheless have been his intent but that he wanted to keep it secret. This is not very credible. There is one tantalizing incident reported in Mark according to which Jesus asked his disciples who people were saying that he was (Mark 8:27–30): "Jesus went on with his disciples to the villages of Caesarea Philippi; and on the way he asked his disciples, 'Who do people say that I am?' [28] And they answered him, 'John the Baptist; and others, Eli-jah; and still others, one of the prophets.' [29] He asked them, 'But who do you say that I am?' Peter answered him, 'You are the Messiah.' [30] And he sternly ordered them not to tell anyone about him" (Mark 8:27–30). They reply: Elijah, a prophet (like Moses), or John the Baptist (on the belief that the executed John was making a reappearance). Asked what they, themselves, thought, Peter as the spokesperson and leader of the disciples replied: "You are the Anointed (= Hebrew: Messiah; Greek: Christ). Jesus immediately instructed them to keep it to themselves.

This may have been Mark's way of explaining why the matter was absent in the material he presented and so reflected not history but Mark's own beliefs. It may, however, reflect Jesus' actual response, knowing how dangerous the notion of messiahship was. For the Messiah, the Christ, usually meant the one people expected to fulfill the hope of a ruler from the house of David who would liberate Israel from its enemies (and that meant Rome!) and establish a kingdom of peace and goodness. To have the rumor spread that Jesus was claiming to be the Messiah would be courting danger. The Romans would crack down on him and have him executed as a rebel, as they had done and would do to others — and did exactly that with him, as we know.

The incident is interesting also for Peter's response in the conversation which follows. For Mark has Jesus go on to predict that he as Son of Man would suffer before finally being vindicated by resurrection: "Then he began to teach them that the Son of Man must undergo great suffering, and be rejected by the elders, the chief priests, and the scribes, and be killed, and after three days rise again. [32]He said all this quite openly. And Peter took him aside and began to rebuke him. [33]But turning and looking at his disciples, he rebuked Peter and said, 'Get behind me, Satan! For you are setting your mind not on divine things but on human things'" (Mark 8:31–33). Based on the usual understanding of royal messiahship, Peter found Jesus' prediction unacceptable. Messiahs win. They don't lose. His response received a sharp rebuke from Jesus. Peter clearly got it wrong but not surprisingly. It was a problematic notion.

Our earliest evidence, which includes instructions given only for the disciples, never takes being Messiah as a theme, so that, if Jesus entertained it, it clearly remained marginal. If he used a self-designation at all, beside his profiling himself as a prophet in bringing healing and hope, it could be the title "Son of Man," with which Mark has him identify himself frequently. He does so, however, primarily with a focus on his authority in judgement and his own vindication (8:38), not on notions of messianic rule. Thus, Mark uses it of his authority to forgive sins (2:10) and to interpret sabbath law: "the Son of Man is lord even of the sabbath" (2:28).

His trial before the Sanhedrin, as Mark depicts it, has him asked about messiahship and the temple, two themes often linked in Jewish hope, as they had been from David's time onwards: "Again the high priest asked him, 'Are you the Messiah, the Son of the Blessed One?' [62]Jesus said, 'I am; and "you will see the Son of Man seated at the right hand of the Power," and "coming with the clouds of heaven"'" (Mark 14:61–62). "Messiah" and "Son of the Blessed," meaning "Son of God," were standard titles for the royal messianic figure. His reply is "yes," but, as in Mark 8, he immediately shifts to speak of himself as the Son of Man, with allusions to the figure in Dan 7, enclosed in the quotation marks.

The Jewish trial may been a historical construct on Mark's part, based on what trials of believers were like in his own time. The fourth Gospel, often preserving useful historical data beneath its imaginative portrayal, mentions no such trial. It is hard to imagine, however, that the messiahship issues had not in some way come up during Jesus' ministry, at least through popular speculation, especially in his last days. His entry into Jerusalem, if historical, however small-scale, was suggestive, and his behavior in one small corner of the massive temple courtyard in overturning the tables of the money changers was at least provocative.

Pilate had his sources. It is hard to account for his action without them. Jesus' disciples' subsequent acclamation of his messiahship is scarcely credible had he resisted the notion to the end. Any such admission, however reticent and redefined beyond its usual meaning, would have left him vulnerable.

As we know, it did. Pilate executed Jesus in the usual way, crucifixion, designed as a gruesome deterrent to all who passed by and watched the agony and the birds pecking out eyes and dogs pulling meat off legs. We can hardly miss the point of Pilate's intent when he puts Jesus between two insurgents (sometimes harmlessly and wrongly called "thieves") and set above him the accusation, "King of the Jews," a description of what messiahship normally meant.

Clearly, he did not see Jesus as head of an armed uprising; otherwise, he would have rounded up the disciples, too, for execution. He saw him nevertheless as belonging in the category of rebellion against Rome's reign and as inciting anti-Roman aspirations. The pungency of preaching the coming of God's empire is easily lost when we fail to recognize that the word usually translated "kingdom" also means "empire." For Pilate, Jesus and Barabbas, who were both dangerous in different ways, were best removed by imprisonment or execution for the sake of peace.

Jesus as Messiah to Come and the *Christianoi*

From the margins, then, in the ministry of Jesus according to our earliest sources, the myth of divine kingship, at least as royal messianic hope, came to center stage. It is there atop the cross in the mocking sign that labeled him "King of the Jews." Executed as the would-be Messiah/Christ, his designation would become the central designation of a movement, Christianity. Locals in Antioch, according to Luke, were first to refer to his followers as *Christianoi* (Acts 11:26). What was at the margins became the center.

Reconstructing what emerged in the wake of Jesus' execution is fraught with difficulty, including what his followers did with what Pilate had moved from the margins to the center, namely the image of Jesus as Messiah, as Christ. The evidence is clear that they did not reject the allegation and plead that he was not claiming to be the Messiah, the Christ, and so had been crucified on false pretenses. Informed by their hopes, which included divine intervention through resurrection and judgement, the coming reign of God, central to Jesus' message, and by their experiences, they concluded that God had raised Jesus from the dead in a transformed state of being in which he had appeared to some of them. This was, at the very least, a sign of God's approval.

These claims of Jesus' vindication by God entailed both confirmation of what he preached, but also confirmation that he was indeed the Messiah, the Christ. What then did that mean? How would he be the Messiah, the Christ?

Luke offers us an answer both in the way he retells the early history in Acts and the way he introduces his Gospel. Among his most striking passages is one where he recreates what he imagined Peter would have said to the crowds. It was best practice of ancient historians to recreate speeches as closely as possible to what they believed would have been said. Peter's speech comes to its climax with a call to repentance: "[19]Repent therefore, and turn to God so that your sins may be wiped out, [20]so that times of refreshing may come from the presence of the Lord, and that he may send the Messiah appointed for you, that is, Jesus, [21]who must remain in heaven until the time of universal restoration that God announced long ago through his holy prophets" (Acts 3:19–21). According to Peter's speech, Jesus was to come in future to play the role of the Messiah, the Christ. This coheres with what we read elsewhere in Luke. He introduces his Gospel with accounts of faithful Jews longing for Israel's liberation through the coming of the Messiah. Mary's song, the *Magnificat*, praises God for the promise of change (1:46–55) and Zechariah blesses God in his *Benedictus*: "Blessed be the Lord God of Israel, for he has looked favorably on his people and redeemed them. [69]He has raised up a mighty savior for us in the house of his servant David, [70]as he spoke through the mouth of his holy prophets from of old, [71]that we would be saved from our enemies and from the hand of all who hate us" (Luke 1:68–71). Similarly, Luke depicts Simeon and Anna as devout Jews also longing for Israel's and Jerusalem's liberation (2:25–38). So, too, Joseph of Arimathea, who was "waiting expectantly for the kingdom of God" (23:51). Luke has Jesus, himself, speak of his return to Jerusalem in the end time, bringing liberation (21:28), to be hailed with the words, "Blessed is the one who comes in the name of the Lord" (13:35). Not surprisingly Luke has the two disciples on the Emmaus Road express disappointment: "we had hoped that he was the one to redeem Israel" (24:21), only to reassured by Jesus about the timing: first the Messiah had to suffer (24:26).

Acts begins with the disciples asking Jesus about these hopes: "Lord, is this the time when you will restore the kingdom to Israel?" (1:6), to which Jesus replies: "It is not for you to know the times or periods that the Father has set by his own authority. ⁸But you will receive power when the Holy Spirit has come upon you; and you will be my witnesses in Jerusalem, in all Judea and Samaria, and to the ends of the earth" (Acts 1:7–8). According to Luke, then, Jesus was telling the disciples that their hopes for his return as Messiah/Christ to rule God's kingdom from a base in Jerusalem were not awry. They just needed more patience. Jesus would come and reign as royal Messiah, as the Christ.

When Luke recreates speeches for his history of that early period, he was able to incorporate traditions known to him which had been foundational for the way those first believers understood Jesus as Messiah. This includes their use of those ancient texts found in the Psalms and elsewhere which adapted the myth of divine kingship and applied it to the Davidic dynasty. One of the earliest interpretations of Jesus' resurrection, aside from it being a vindication of all that Jesus claimed, was to see it as the act whereby God appointed Jesus as the Messiah, the Christ to come.

The most cited and alluded-to text of the Old Testament in the New Testament is accordingly Psalm 110:1. "The LORD says to my lord, 'Sit at my right hand until I make your enemies your footstool.'" Accordingly, Acts reports Peter as declaring the following:

> Being therefore exalted at the right hand of God, and having received from the Father the promise of the Holy Spirit, he has poured out this that you both see and hear. ³⁴For David did not ascend into the heavens, but he himself says, "The Lord said to my Lord, 'Sit at my right hand, ³⁵until I make your enemies your footstool.' ³⁶Therefore let the entire house of Israel know with certainty that God has made him both Lord and Messiah, this Jesus whom you crucified." (Acts 2:33–36)

The same thought recurs in Acts 5, again on the lips of Peter: "The God of our ancestors raised up Jesus, whom you had killed by hanging him on a tree. [31]God exalted him at his right hand as Leader and Savior, so that he might give repentance to Israel and forgiveness of sins" (Acts 5:30–31). Another of the ancient texts where we see the myth of divine kingship adapted is in Ps 2: "I will tell of the decree of the LORD: He said to me, 'You are my son; today I have begotten you. [8]Ask of me, and I will make the nations your heritage, and the ends of the earth your possession. [9]You shall break them with a rod of iron, and dash them in pieces like a potter's vessel'" (Ps 2:7–9). Luke has Paul cite Psalm 2:7 in Acts 13:33. The author of Hebrews assembles a collection of quotations from such psalms to hail Jesus as Messiah. He frames them with an allusion to Psalm 110:1 (1:3) and an actual citation of it (1:13). His first citation is then Psalm 2:7 about Jesus as God's Son, one of his key themes as he sets Jesus above the angels (1:5). "For to which of the angels did God ever say, 'You are my Son; today I have begotten you'?"

He then cites another Psalm emanating from adaptation of the divine kingship myth: "Of the angels he says, 'He makes his angels winds, and his servants flames of fire' [Psalm 104:4]. [8]But of the Son he says, 'Your throne, O God, is for ever and ever, and the righteous scepter is the scepter of your kingdom. [9]You have loved righteousness and hated wickedness; therefore God, your God, has anointed you with the oil of gladness beyond your companions'" (Psalm 45:8; cf. Hebrews 1:7–9). "Throne, scepter, anointing" were all central to coronation ritual. The author of Hebrews is probably alluding to Psalm 89:22, when in 1:6 he refers to Jesus becoming God's "firstborn," being brought "into the world," brought to birth, adopted, at his enthronement: "And again, when he brings the firstborn into the world, he says, 'Let all God's angels worship him' (Psalm 97:7)." He also goes beyond the Psalms to include another text reflecting adaptation of the divine kingship myth, namely the prophet Nathan's oracle of God's promise about David's son, Solomon, in 2 Samuel 7:14: "I will be his Father, and he will be my Son" (Hebrews 1:5).

Some decades earlier we find Paul citing early Christian confessions which also include such allusions. Thus, in Romans 1 he cites what his hearers would recognize as the belief they shared in common with him about Jesus: "the gospel concerning his Son, who was descended from David according to the flesh [4]and was declared to be Son of God with power according to the spirit of holiness by resurrection from the dead, Jesus Christ our Lord" (Romans 1:3–5). Framed within this adaptation of the divine kingship myth, applied to the hope for a Messiah, and so applied to Jesus as Messiah, this confession declares that Jesus was appointed Son of God at his resurrection. A more literal translation makes this clearer: "was appointed Son of God according to the spirit of holiness from the [his] resurrection from the dead."

Paul, too, cites Psalm 110:1, using it to explain the meaning of Christ's resurrection. Thus, in Romans 8 he writes: "Who will bring any charge against God's elect? It is God who justifies. [34]Who is to condemn? It is Christ Jesus, who died, yes, who was raised, who is at the right hand of God, who indeed intercedes for us" (Romans 8:33–34). He uses the same tradition in 1 Corinthians 15 where he combines the allusion to Psalm 110:1, of Christ being enthroned at God's right hand, with Psalm 8:7, a text originally about human beings but now applied directly to Christ: For "God has put all things in subjection under his feet." But when it says, "All things are put in subjection," it is plain that this does not include the one who put all things in subjection under him. [28]When all things are subjected to him, then the Son himself will also be subjected to the one who put all things in subjection under him, so that God may be all in all" (1 Corinthians 15:27–28). We find the combination of Psalm 110:1 and Psalm 8:7 to speak of Christ's enthronement as Messiah also in Hebrews where both are directly cited (1:13; 2:6–7), but also behind other texts like 1 Peter, which refers to "the resurrection of Jesus Christ, [22]who has gone into heaven and is at the right hand of God, with angels, authorities, and powers made subject to him" (1 Peter 3:21–22) and Ephesians where we read:

> God put this power to work in Christ when he raised him from the dead and seated him at his right hand in the heavenly places, [21]far above all rule and authority and power and dominion, and above every name that is named, not only in this age but also in the age to come. [22]And he has put all things under his feet and has made him the head over all things for the church, [23]which is his body, the fullness of him who fills all in all. (Ephesians 1:20–23)

The allusion to Jesus being seated at God's right hand as an interpretation of his resurrection was thus widespread. It symbolized one of the major ways in which people described Jesus' significance. In some ways it is best to see it as a code or a certain framework of thought. Colossians includes a passage in poetic style in two parts. The second part draws on some of the motifs of kingship ideology adapted to apply to Jesus' role in the church since his resurrection describing him as "the head of the body, the church; he is the beginning, the firstborn from the dead" (1:18).

Israel's adaptation of the myth of divine kingship could not make kings into gods but could employ motifs which belonged to kingship ideology. It would have been felt to be important for purposes of propaganda and control to make the most of it. Accordingly, the anointed king was adopted as God's son at his enthronement. He was in that sense God's Anointed Son of God by adoption as well as a descendant of David. Naturally when people longed for a return of a king of David's line, they used the same motifs. Accordingly, some of the key texts belonging to kingship ideology reappear in their expressions of hope.

When they declared Jesus to be the fulfillment of these hopes, they similarly used royal kingship ideology. Jesus, accordingly, was the hoped-for Son of David. He was the Anointed, the Messiah, the Christ. At his resurrection he was exalted to God's right hand and enthroned as God's Son, God's firstborn Son. He would return to be the ruler of God's kingdom on earth, probably, as Luke indicates, based in Jerusalem.

It is important to see how early traditions linked Messiah and Son of God as equivalent designations of royal status. We saw this in Mark's account of Jesus' trial before the Sanhedrin, where Mark has the high priest ask: "Are you the Christ, the Son of the Blessed One?" (14:61). By Mark's day, however, "Son of God" had come to mean much more and so he has the high priest accuse Jesus of blasphemy. There was nothing blasphemous in claiming to be God's Messiah, God's Son, the Anointed. There were many who claimed to be Messiah and they were not charged with blasphemy. The way that believers in Mark's day, however, spoke of Jesus as Son of God had come to mean much more than it had done when used in royal ideology and messianic hope. Luke was sensitive to this and so separated the high priest's question into two different questions, one about messiahship and one about being Son of God.

Matthew's version of Peter's acclamation of Jesus as the Messiah, adds "the Son of the living God" (16:16). The connection between messiahship and sonship comes through also in John's Gospel where Nathanael declares: "'Rabbi, you are the Son of God! You are the King of Israel!'" (1:49). In many instances in the fourth Gospel "Son of God" still occurs where there is a link between the title and the notion of Jesus as Messiah and traditional roles associated with it, including roles of the Son of Man, as in 1:50–51, and reflecting the link between messiahship and the Son of Man figure in the Parables of Enoch noted above. Accordingly, he is called Son of God where roles of the Son of Man as judge occur (5:25–27; 9:35–39). Martha's response to Jesus connects the two: "She said to him, 'Yes, Lord, I believe that you are the Messiah, the Son of God, the one coming into the world'" (11:27). Confessing Jesus as the Christ was a standard way of coming to faith and so occurs in the summary of the gospel: "But these are written so that you may come to believe that Jesus is the Messiah, the Son of God, and that through believing you may have life in his name" (20:31). Far more common in John is the simple designation of Jesus as "the Son," which carried with it a much wider world of meaning as we shall see in the next chapter.

Expanding the Messiahship Model

It made very good sense for Jews of Palestine and abroad, longing for liberation, to hail Jesus as their Messiah. It had, however, its limitations. Would members of other nations be so interested in hopes for a Jewish Messiah and a kingdom based in Palestine? We see a transition and development which moved beyond the royal messianic model. That included that the passing of time probably brought greater focus to Jesus' present status in the heavenly world.

Instead of waiting in the interim for a short time to pass before he reappeared, and occasionally asking God to help his followers in their struggles as intercessor, Jesus might be seen to be already exercising rule on God's behalf. That was a much broader and universal understanding of his dominion where the chief enemies to be overcome were not the Romans and their agents in Palestine, but demons and powerful angels. This entailed a shift at least of focus from his coming to establish his reign on earth to his reigning with God in heaven, and so to hail him as king and Lord became not so much an expression of hope of what might one day be but what currently is. "Christ" was beginning to fill with new meaning both in terms of how people understood his reign and also how they then saw his death and then his life as reflecting this status.

The motif of royal messiahship remained, as it were, firmly connected with Jesus' death. It was the title affixed to the cross as a mocking accusation: "King of the Jews," the Jews' Messiah. Belief in Jesus' resurrection re-established hope because it was the proof that God had vindicated Jesus, affirming his message, and had, indeed, now appointed him to be the Messiah to come. It meant, however, even more than that. His early followers began to see in his death more than humiliation followed by exaltation. They saw in his death exemplary suffering such as the Psalms, especially Ps 22, foreshadowed and so described the event using its imagery.

Israel's traditions, however, could see even more in such suffering and martyrdom than just exemplary obedience. For the martyrs killed in the Maccabean uprising 167–164 BCE were seen as creating a surplus of goodness sufficient to cover not only any sins of their own, but also the sins of others. And already the prophet whose words now fill Isaiah 40–55 could speak of God's servant, perhaps originally an image of Israel, itself, as similarly undergoing suffering which brought benefit for others (Isaiah 53). This could surely also be so of Jesus, the Christ, and so we find early confessional material declaring: "Christ (the Messiah) died for us" or "Christ died for our sins." This let loose cultic imagination to translate this affirmation into a diversity of forms which spoke of Jesus' death as therefore functioning as a sacrifice. It opened a wide range of options of seeing Jesus as like a daily sacrifice, a special sacrifice, an atoning sacrifice, as like the Passover lamb linked to celebration of liberation, and much more.

In time, what was already an element of Jewish faith, and central to John the Baptist's proclamation and Jesus' ministry—namely, forgiveness of sins—became attached above all to his death. In that sense, it helped redefine royal messiahship away from notions of victory over Israel's enemies and toward liberation from sin and its consequences, salvation in a much broader sense. As such, it would have more universal appeal, especially when combined with notions of universal judgement. This was another creative adaptation and redeployment of the myth of divine kingship, already going beyond anything associated with royal kingship or royal messianic hopes. The fact that he died accused of having aspirations of messiahship under the heading of "King of the Jews" played a significant part in this development.

The change of focus from the prospect of an earthly messianic reign at his coming to his present exalted heavenly state had significant implications. So also did the development of profound reflections on his impact generally and his death, in particular, as creating a surplus of benefit for others. It unleashed an array of imagery, not least images associated with sacrifice, because it was commonly held that sacrifices also created such benefit. These two developments, the focus on the heavenly, rather than the earthly rule of Jesus as Messiah and the extrapolation of understandings of his death as "for sins," "for us," expanded and in a sense exploded traditional notions of messiahship.

Filled with new meaning this designation, Christ, could now become the frame for understanding also his ministry. His role as the Christ, the Messiah, did not begin only after his death. It began in his ministry, well-attested in circulating anecdotes and sayings being told and retold and eventually put into writing. His death, then, was seen not as a meaningless dip and humiliation but paradoxically as a climax rich in meaning. It reflected who he was and what he did in his ministry. Others, like Matthew and Luke, would further extend this to see it reflected in his birth.

While Mark portrays the disciples as hailing Jesus as Messiah only after half the story has been told, namely not until Mark 8 where Peter acclaims him, Mark has framed Jesus' whole story with hints of messianic status. A heavenly voice at his baptism declares: "You are my Son, the Beloved; with you I am well pleased" (1:11), a combination of the words of royal coronation adopting the king from Ps 2:7, "You are my Son; today I have begotten you," and Isaiah 42:1, "Here is my servant, whom I uphold, my chosen, in whom my soul delights; I have put my spirit upon him." Such use of biblical allusions in narrating Jesus' story was typical and reinforced a sense of continuity between God's acts in the past and God's action in Jesus.

Mark makes this declaration at Jesus' baptism the first of three such acclamations which frame his Gospel. Doing things in sets of three was typical of the rhetoric of the times. The second acclamation echoes the first and comes in another intervention from on high which embroiders the story. Thus, at his transfiguration, where Jesus is depicted as transformed into the shining figure people expected him to be at his return, the voice of God is heard again through the clouds: "This is my Son, the Beloved; listen to him!" (9:7). In the context which had included Peter's confession of Jesus as the Christ, the Messiah, there had been reference to Elijah and the prophet like Moses (8:27–29). Both of them appear on the scene in the transfiguration. The reference to Jesus as "Son" will again reflect, at least in part, Jesus' status as Messiah, Son of God, as in kingship ideology.

The third acclamation comes as a climax when the gentile centurion declares at the cross, "Truly this man was God's Son!" (15:39). The point is hardly to be missed that Mark celebrates here the mission to the gentiles among whom the faith in his time was now spreading. Luke, who had his own plan to speak of the mission to the gentiles through his second volume in Acts, reduces it to admiration of innocence, having the centurion observe: "Certainly this man was innocent" (Luke 23:47).

Mark not only has such messianic acclamations made from above. He also has them made from below, namely on the lips of demons who, they would have assumed, would know Jesus' special identity and address him accordingly as "the Holy One of God": "What have you to do with us, Jesus of Nazareth? Have you come to destroy us? I know who you are, the Holy One of God" (1:25). Similarly, Mark reports that such spirits "fell down before him and shouted, 'You are the Son of God!' [12]But he sternly ordered them not to make him known" (3:12) and that the Gerasene demoniac cried out, "What have you to do with me, Jesus, Son of the Most High God? I adjure you by God, do not torment me" (5:7). Already in these instances we see a shift in employment of the royal messianic idea from overcoming Israel's enemies to overcoming the demonic, a key theme in Mark's portrait of Jesus and his role.

Mark retains the allusions to Israel's adaptation of the divine kingship myth in having Jesus speak of his return as Son of Man/Messiah when asked about messiahship by the high priest before the Sanhedrin. He has Jesus declare, combining the imagery of Psalm 110:1 and Daniel 7:13, "you will see the Son of Man seated at the right hand of the Power, and coming with the clouds of heaven" (14:62). That future role, however, no longer relates to establishing a Jerusalem based kingdom as Luke still has it, but, as Mark puts it in his depiction of Jesus' predictions about the future,

> In those days, after that suffering, the sun will be darkened, and the moon will not give its light, [25]and the stars will be falling from heaven, and the powers in the heavens will be shaken. [26]Then they will see "the Son of Man coming in clouds" with great power and glory. [27]Then he will send out the angels, and gather his elect from the four winds, from the ends of the earth to the ends of heaven. (Mark 13:24–27)

For Mark, to see Jesus as Israel's Messiah, as "Son of David," as blind Bartimaeus acclaims him (10:47–48), followed by the crowds at his entry, crying "Blessed is the coming kingdom of our ancestor David! Hosanna in the highest heaven!" (11:9–10), is not enough. He even has Jesus play off Psalm 110:1 against its inadequacy, arguing that "The Lord said to my lord" has to mean more than Davidic messiahship. Assuming David authored the Psalm as people did, he declares, "David himself calls him Lord; so how can he be his son?" (12:37). For Mark and Mark's hearers, who would have included many with no connection to Israel, Jesus' significance was no longer to be confined to Jewish messianic expectation of royal kingship. Jesus was more than that. Christ was Lord in a much broader sense.

"Lord" lent itself to wider use beyond notions of kingship and royal ideology for it opened wider perspectives on Jesus' role and status. Deities in cults were acclaimed as lords and equally significant, the Hebrew of God's name, YHWH, was often replaced in Greek translation with the term "Lord," reflecting how people avoided pronouncing the divine name by using the Hebrew word meaning "Lord." People were familiar with the practice of asking another to act in one's name, meaning with your authority and permission. They could also speak of someone bearing another's name in that sense, especially when speaking of God authorizing kings to be their vice regents on earth. It also had the potential to go beyond such notions of kingship. Paul, indeed, cites a hymnic passage which envisages that in the resurrection God gave Jesus his name: "Therefore God also highly exalted him and gave him the name that is above every name, [10]so that at the name of Jesus every knee should bend, in heaven and on earth and under the earth, [11]and every tongue should confess that Jesus Christ is Lord, to the glory of God the Father" (Philippians 2:9–11). Mark, thus, goes beyond royal messiahship, preferring to have Jesus speak of himself as Son of Man and depicting Jesus' mission, as defined by John the Baptist, as baptizing with the Spirit (1:8). By this he meant liberating people by the power of the Spirit from evil spirits, not leading the nation to victory over Rome as the enemy. This rendered the story of Jesus relevant far beyond its original setting among Jewish hopes and aspirations and spoke to the non-Jewish world.

Matthew, too, provides a framework around his story of Jesus which emphasizes his messiahship already during his ministry. Accordingly, he adds opening chapters which do so through legends about Jesus' miraculous birth. Luke does similarly. Both found inspiration in the wisp of hope announced by Isaiah to the nervous southern kingdom of Judah after the Assyrians had overrun the northern kingdom of Israel in the late eighth century. That hope was that Judah would soon be rescued from its fears, in as little time as a young married woman became pregnant and gave birth. The prophet suggests that such a child be called Emmanuel, meaning "God is with us." God would be with them.

The Hebrew text bringing divine comfort read, "Therefore the Lord himself will give you a sign. Look, the young woman is with child and shall bear a son, and shall name him Immanuel" (Isaiah 7:14). Its Greek translation used a word for young woman which normally meant "virgin" and so lent itself to support the emerging stories of Jesus being miraculously created to be God's agent the Messiah. This has its parallel in the account of the miraculous conception of Melchizedek in 2 Enoch 71–71, one step beyond the miraculous tales of postmenopausal women like Sarah in her nineties giving birth to Isaac. It certainly fitted to depict Jesus as representing the fact that God is with us and can bear the name Emmanuel. Matthew has this echoed in the closing words of his Gospel when he has Jesus promise that he would be always with the disciples to the end of the age (28:20).

Matthew also provides a genealogy of Jesus tracing his descent from Abraham through King David. He even gives it a structure based on the number fourteen. That is a hidden allusion to David, because in Hebrew consonants also served as numbers and the consonants making up David's name added up to fourteen! Matthew also depicts Jesus as born under the messianic star promised in Numbers 17:24: "A star shall arise in Jacob, a scepter in Israel."

Matthew follows Mark in retelling the threefold acclamation of Jesus as Son of God at his baptism and transfiguration and on the lips of a centurion at his death. Peter's confession, however, is not as in Mark the first sign that the disciples acclaim Jesus' messiahship. He has them do so when they see Jesus walking on water (14:33). He is also more restrained about portraying the demons as acknowledging Jesus, limiting it to just the Gadarene demoniacs.

Indeed, Matthew shows less interest in portraying Jesus as an exorcist. He even omits Mark's opening scene of the exorcism in the synagogue (Mark 1:21–28). He focuses instead on Jesus as teacher, extracting from that story only the statement about Jesus' teaching authority and making it the climax of the sermon on the mount: "Now when Jesus had finished saying these things, the crowds were astounded at his teaching, [29]for he taught them as one having authority, and not as their scribes" (7:28–29). In Mark it read: "They were astounded at his teaching, for he taught them as one having authority, and not as the scribes" (1:22).

For Matthew Jesus was above all to be seen as the sole authoritative teacher of God's law. Teaching was also sometimes seen as a role to be exercised by the Messiah. The focus on Jesus as teacher was also closely associated with his understanding of Jesus as Son of Man, who would come to lead the day of judgement on the basis of the law. In Matthew this does not deny Jesus' messiahship. It rather redefines it in ways that reflect some similarity with the image of the Son of Man figure in the Parables of Enoch, where the Son of Man has royal messianic traits. Matthew's Jesus is not the savior to liberate Israel from its oppressors. Rather he is to be their savior from sin (1:21). In part this looks forward to his death understood in his tradition as atoning for sin (26:28), but it also encompasses his ministry of bringing God's forgiveness in acts of healing (9:6) and, as in Judaism, teaching his disciples to pray for forgiveness (6:12, 14). It also fitted well his role as judge to come as announced by John the Baptist (3:10–12), who so emphasizes this role that he must send his disciples to be reassured that what Jesus was doing in his ministry cohered with his role as Messiah and judge to come, as Matthew tells us in 11:2–6.

Luke, too, provides a framework around his story of Jesus which emphasizes his messiahship already during his ministry and, like Matthew, adds opening chapters which do so through legends about Jesus' miraculous birth. As we have seen, Luke retains the traditional hopes associated with royal messianic expectation and envisages Jesus returning to earth to fulfill that role. He makes that clear already in the first two chapters of his Gospel. There, devout Jews long for the Messiah and Luke, like Matthew, hails Jesus miraculous conception as God's creative act to fulfill their hope.

For Luke, too, this raised the question of how he saw Jesus' ministry as the Messiah, the Anointed One, before his exaltation to that role at God's right hand after his death. Luke depicts it using what once a prophet, whose works now form the final chapters of the book of Isaiah, had said of his own role (Isaiah 61:1). Luke has Jesus make them his own with a little adaptation in his own home synagogue. Accordingly, he declares: "The Spirit of the Lord is upon me, because he has anointed me to bring good news to the poor. He has sent me to proclaim release to the captives and recovery of sight to the blind, to let the oppressed go free, [19]to proclaim the year of the Lord's favor" (Luke 4:16–19). The focus is twofold. "Good news for the poor," addresses Israel in its need as "the poor" and looks to the future role of the Messiah as traditionally understood and defined in Luke's opening chapters. In addition, however, secondly, in the interim Jesus the Messiah, here specifically as the "Anointed," would engage in acts of healing and liberation. This is strikingly similar to one of the texts found at Qumran, 4Q521/4QMessianic Apocalypse, cited above, which similarly sees acts of healing as a role which the Messiah was to fulfill.

This twofold roles of future hope and present action find confirmation in the chapters which follow. The proclamation of "good news for the poor" meets us in the beatitudes where Jesus declares of the future: "Blessed are you who are poor, for yours is the kingdom of God. [21]Blessed are you who are hungry now, for you will be filled. Blessed are you who weep now, for you will laugh" (Luke 6:20–21). Then, when John the Baptist's disciples fulfill his errand of checking what Jesus was doing and why, Luke depicts Jesus as replying: "Go and tell John what you have seen and heard: the blind receive their sight, the lame walk, the lepers are cleansed, the deaf hear, the dead are raised, the poor have good news brought to them. [23]And blessed is anyone who takes no offence at me" (Luke 7:22–23). Luke had provided evidence of such activity in chapters 4–7.

In John's Gospel the notion of Jesus as royal Messiah features within the account of Jesus' ministry but John goes far beyond its limited scope. As noted above, we still see traces of old connections, such as the use of "Son of God" as belonging to kingship ideology as a designation for the king as God's adopted son, but for John Jesus as Son is a much richer sense fed by different streams of thought, a theme to which we return in the following chapter. The few discussions specifically of messiahship, such as with John the Baptist (1:25; 3:28), the Samaritan woman (4:25, 28), Martha (11:27), the crowds (7:26–31; 9:22; 10:24; 12:34), and as a confession (9:22; 20:31) are subordinated to this larger claim.

In the course of time notions of Jesus as the Messiah, the Christ, which gave his followers their nametag, faded, or became swallowed up in beliefs which transformed it to mean something much more, eventually better expressed by more universal terms. Jesus Christ then no longer highlighted Jesus as the Jewish Messiah but became more like a surname, a not surprising misapprehension over time, which sounded to some ears as though he was Jesus, son of Mr. and Mrs. Christ. For to acclaim Jesus Christ as Lord went far beyond the framework of royal messianic hope.

Another reason for this eclipse of royal ideology as a vehicle for expounding Jesus' significance lay in the need to develop new, more universally relevant ways of speaking about him which not only spoke to a wider audience but also did better justice to the life and ministry of Jesus before his crucifixion.

Correcting the Divine Kingship Model

The myth of divine kingship, however adapted, thus moved from the margins to center stage but then failed to capture Jesus' significance. Its language persisted and persists still but it underwent serious correction which has not always been successful.

The image of a Messiah, a king who would command an army and overthrow the Romans, wearing a crown, holding a scepter and hailed by the masses, hardly fits the figure presented to us in the anecdotes and sayings of Jesus. Nothing suggests he went about seeking adulation. Mark does report his final entry into Jerusalem as one where he was acclaimed, but his tradition of Jesus' last days, drawing on Zechariah and especially Ps 22, has him entering in lowliness seated on a donkey.

Mark, indeed, does much more to counter triumphant images of Jesus. When Peter confessed Jesus as the Christ, Mark makes a special point of exposing Peter's misapprehension of what it meant. Instead of promising victory over enemies Jesus, according to Mark, Jesus speaks of himself as on a path to suffering and execution only then to be raised in vindication by God. Peter's objections meet, as we noted, a rebuke: "Get behind me, Satan! For you are setting your mind not on divine things but on human things" (8:33).

Mark was saying Peter got it wrong not only about Jesus but also about God. Mark is engaged in serious correction of Peter's understanding of Jesus as Messiah and of God. The redirection is already apparent in what immediately follows where Mark has Jesus address the disciples and the crowds about the values that are to characterize his followers. "If any want to become my followers, let them deny themselves and take up their cross and follow me. [35]For those who want to save their life will lose it, and those who lose their life for my sake, and for the sake of the gospel, will save it" (Mark 8:34–35). No place for self-aggrandizement! Real care for self means abandoning such manipulations and being willing, like Jesus himself, to engage in costly living. That costly living put love for others at the center and paradoxically defined that as the way to true self interest, gaining one's life.

Mark pursues this theme in the chapters which follow, where in 9:31 he again indicated his path of lowly suffering (9:31), only to find his disciples obsessed with who among them was the greatest. He confronts them with a child not yet taken up with self-promotion and calls them to humility. The theme returns in Mark 10 where, again, Jesus speaks of his path of suffering and by contrast, James and John lobby Jesus to be given positions of prominence and power in Jesus' coming messianic kingdom. Mark has made the disciples' continuing obsessions laughable.

Mark has Jesus engage in important social observation in a clear differentiation between what the disciples and many think is greatness and what he was advocating about both himself and God. "So Jesus called them and said to them, "You know that among the Gentiles those whom they recognize as their rulers lord it over them, and their great ones are tyrants over them. ⁴³But it is not so among you; but whoever wishes to become great among you must be your servant, ⁴⁴and whoever wishes to be first among you must be slave of all. ⁴⁵For the Son of Man came not to be served but to serve, and to give his life a ransom for many" (Mark 10:42–45). This is a radical correction of notions of greatness embedded in the myth of kingship and its adaptations. It is not, in Mark, an interim arrangement, as though lowly service is temporary or even a precondition for being able to abandon it and lull in glory when it is over. That certainly would have been a possible interpretation of Jesus' enthronement as Messiah at the resurrection and it would effectively undermine the values he had espoused. On the contrary, the love and compassion embodied in what he had done in his ministry remained embodied in his being and was to remain embodied in the being and doing of the disciples.

Even more radical, Mark was making the point that these are also God's priorities which Peter failed to see. Mark opens a window to enable us to view God not as a projection of human obsessions with power and self-aggrandizement, but as characterized by goodness and love. In this way Jesus, too, had spoken of the kingdom of God, God's reign, as bringing hope and healing.

The myth of divine kingship and its adaptations thus underwent a remake, based on the actions and teaching of Jesus, in which those strands of Israel's faith which lauded God's goodness and compassion came to the fore: "As a father has compassion for his children, so the LORD has compassion for those who fear him. ¹⁴For he knows how we were made; he remembers that we are dust" (Psalm 103:13). Or as Hosea hears God speaking as a loving parent: "How can I give you up, Ephraim? How can I hand you over, O Israel? How can I make you like Admah? How can I treat you like Zeboiim? My heart recoils within me; my compassion grows warm and tender" (Hosea 11:8). There was something stronger than the tendency to create God in the image of rulers. Accordingly, Jesus told the parable of the loving father and wayward son (Luke 15:11–32) and across so many anecdotes emerges as one who depicts God as putting compassion first and confronting hate and self-importance.

Mark's demolition of traditional kingship reaches its climax in his depiction of Jesus, King of the Jews, Messiah, enthroned on a cross and crowned with a crown of thorns. This is deliberately subversive of what were common values. John's Gospel makes the same point in its own way in having Jesus wash his disciples' feet (13:1–20).

Engaging the Myth of Divine Kingship

What are we to do with the myth of divine kingship and its adaptations which Israelites brought in from the margins to create a dynasty and followers of Jesus came to bear proudly as their label, Christians? Its influence persists. Many people love power. Many people want to be the center of attention or want adulation. Many people believe greatness is to be the center of adoration. They do so because these are the dominant values that surround them. They do so also out of a dearth of love and self-love which such ambitions seek to compensate.

Such influence corrupts leadership, secular and religious. Its models of greatness which inspired models of thinking of God as all powerful seated on a throne wanting adulation have increasingly been called into question. Politicians who seek self-aggrandizement lose respect. Genuine honor and respect go to those who exhibit goodness, generosity, and compassion.

Sadly, it became possible to co-opt Jesus to become the patron of those seeking power and adulation. Artists could paint him looking just like the powerful. Hailed for his bravery like heroes of old he becomes so easily the symbol of a system which values achievement and success, the winners and achievers, those who deserve adulation and to be loved, in contrast to the rest, deemed lesser beings and undeserving. Such hero worship of Jesus subverts what he lived and died for. If our imagination allows it, we might see the masses, the unworthy, the sinners, the tax collectors, and find Jesus not elevated among the elite looking down upon them but in their midst deeming them all worthy of love and care. The myth of divine kingship becomes a monster which crushes hope and crucifies him again.

Christian communities are caught in a paradox of asserting gospel values of love and compassion while operating within liturgical traditions based on court rituals which put adoration of power and acts of obeisance before it at the forefront in spirit if not in deed. We sing hymns and songs of adoration shaped and inspired by the acclamation of monarchs long after we have abolished their pretense or had them reduced to symbolism.

I find myself living in a disconnect between what the gospel affirms and the words I sing and say in ancient liturgies, reluctant to abandon the one or the other. When I sing, "O worship the king, all glorious above," I disavow the surface meaning and engage in deep connection in my being with the one who gives life and meaning and hope. I am used to doing so but as a liturgist I am also alert to the dangers or seek to be. For I am intoning values I resist, using language I reject, echoing values which I know have allowed the myth of divine kingship and its adaptations to remain central and pollute the faith I hold dear. Aesthetics then win over intellect.

The situation is not, however, hopeless. Prayers and hymns, let alone preaching and public reflection, can be better attuned to the gospel and need, indeed, to be exposed where they are. Some compromise is inevitable, but I remind myself how easy it is to betray the faith and betray it for others.

Part of the hope lies in the fact that there is more to the tradition than adaptations of the myth of kingship. There are traditions older than kingship and wider than the notions of messiahship it embodied. Hiding on the margins is promise of universal meaning and hope which shed better light on God and faith.

4

The Myth of Wisdom Sophia

Don't go lusting after immoral women! Make Wisdom your lover
instead and embrace all she offers!

WHAT BEGAN ON THE margins as sage advice to young men would feed
into the myth of Wisdom as a woman and from there become a significant
tributary to the stream of thought which generated amongst other things
the doctrine of the Trinity. This chapter will trace that stream of thought, its
journey from the margins to the center of Christian faith.

Men, Behave!

The instructions and reflections assembled together in the book of Proverbs include strong advice to young married men, especially in Proverbs
1–9. Proverbs, a collection of wisdom sayings, bears the name of Solomon,
the legendary wise king who lived half a millennium earlier. It was typical
of compositions of the time to attribute their origin to great figures of the
past, such as attributing the first five books of the Bible, Genesis to Deuteronomy, to Moses, and accounts of heavenly visions to Enoch.

The author of Proverbs, claiming to speak as "Solomon" or at least
in his name, warns men to beware of "the loose women . . . the adulteress with her smooth words, [17]who forsakes the partner of her youth and
forgets her sacred covenant; [18]for her way leads down to death" (2:16–18).
In chapter 5 the advice continues: "And now, my child, listen to me, and
do not depart from the words of my mouth. [8]Keep your way far from
her, and do not go near the door of her house" (Prov 5:7–8). It becomes
very specific: "Drink water from your own cistern, flowing water from
your own well. [16]Should your springs be scattered abroad, streams of

water in the streets? ¹⁷Let them be for yourself alone, and not for sharing with strangers. ¹⁸Let your fountain be blessed, and rejoice in the wife of your youth, ¹⁹a lovely deer, a graceful doe. May her breasts satisfy you at all times; may you be intoxicated always by her love. ²⁰Why should you be intoxicated, my son, by another woman and embrace the bosom of an adulteress?" (Proverbs 5:15–20).

This is very explicit imagery. Drinking from one's own well is about sexual intercourse with one's own wife. The man's fount is his penis and scattering his springs is spilling his semen elsewhere, sowing his wild oats, as we might say. Such advice continues in the chapters which follow, warning of the seductive words and attire of the wayward woman, the vengeance of the betrayed husband, and they even describe scenes of seduction, of women luring men into sexual wrongdoing:

> "Come, let us take our fill of love until morning; let us delight ourselves with love. ¹⁹For my husband is not at home; he has gone on a long journey . . ." With much seductive speech she persuades him; with her smooth talk she compels him. ²²Right away he follows her, and goes like an ox to the slaughter, or bounds like a stag towards the trap ²³until an arrow pierces its entrails. He is like a bird rushing into a snare, not knowing that it will cost him his life. (Proverbs 7:18–23)

The author depicts the "foolish woman" as sitting at the door of her house and calling out, "'You who are simple, turn in here!' And to those without sense she says, ¹⁷'Stolen water is sweet, and bread eaten in secret is pleasant.' ¹⁸But they do not know that the dead are there, that her guests are in the depths of Sheol" (Proverbs 9:16–18). The advice is addressed to men behaving badly. It had the potential to put all the blame on the women but clearly it seeks also to hold men to account. It was as relevant then as it is in every age. It is male discourse and appeals to what is in men's self-interest and what may bring them harm and, typically of the time, says nothing about what might be in the interests of women and what dangers and harm, let alone abuse, they might suffer.

Those who translated these passages into the Greek version of the Old Testament retained the focus, though toned down the explicit references at times, such as the reference to the man's penis as a fountain and sexual intercourse with one's wife as drinking from a well and it deletes reference to the loose woman found in 2:16–18, cited above. The translators appear also to depict the woman as a foreigner, perhaps reflecting the situation of the diaspora where many saw foreign women as potentially corrupting. The warnings about adultery remain in parts, especially now supplemented in chapter 9 with additional detail about the folly of the adulterer: "He who supports himself with lies will as well herd winds, and the same person will pursue flying birds, for he has forsaken the ways of his vineyard and has caused the axles on his own farm to go astray. Yes he travels through an arid wilderness and a land destined for drought, and gathers barrenness with his hands" (Proverbs 9:12).

Another supplement spells out what a man confronted with the danger of adultery (drinking from a strange well) should do: "Run away; do not linger in the place, neither fix your eye upon her, for so you will cross strange water and pass through a strange river. However, abstain from strange water, and do not drink from a strange well, that you may live for a long time and years of life may be added to you" (Proverbs 9:18a–d). Among the scrolls found in the Dead Sea caves at Qumran is a document, to which the name "The Wiles of the Wicked Woman" has been given (4Q184). It similarly depicts an immoral woman: "Her heart weaves traps, her kidneys nets. Her eyes have been defiled with evil, her hands grasp the pit, her feet descend to act wickedly, and to walk in crimes . . . [are] foundations of darkness, and there are plenty of sins in her wings [or: in her hems/skirts]" (4Q184 1 2b-4) (*DSSSE* supplemented).

> She has no inheritance among all 8 those who shine [.] brightly. She is the start of all the ways of wickedness. Alas! She is the ruination of all who inherit her, and calamity for a[ll] 9 who grasp her. For her paths are paths of death, and her roads are tracks to sin. Her trails lead astray 10 towards wickedness, and her pathways to the guilt of transgression. Her gates are the gates of death, In the entrance to her house Sheo[l] proceeds. 11 A[l]l [those who go to her will not] come back, and all those who inherit her will descend to the pit. (4Q184 1 7b-11a)

Square brackets indicate where there are gaps in the manuscript and what it probably read. Its warnings echo those in Proverbs.

The words of the sage, Ben Sira, writing in the early second century BCE, picks up the warnings in Proverbs in declaring, "Do not approach a strange woman, lest you fall into her snares" (Ben Sira 9:3), but sets them in a broader context of warnings about jealousy, associating with a prostitute, sleeping with female musicians, looking at virgins, giving oneself to a prostitute, looking at beautiful women, and consorting with married women

(9:1–9). Ben Sira's grandson translates the warnings sometimes with supplement so that to the words: "Wine and women cause the heart/mind [to be loose]" (19:2), he adds: "and one who joins himself to prostitutes will be more reckless." The work assumes that some married women engaged in prostitution, an assumption which may already be traced in Proverbs, which contrasts the cost of paying a prostitute with the cost of adultery with someone's wife plying prostitution: "for a prostitute's fee is only a loaf of bread, but the wife of another stalks a man's very life" (Proverbs 6:26).

Concern with adultery was about more than personal hurt inflicted or experienced. It was very much about the stability of households which were the foundation of the economy and so about the welfare of the community. This is why they arranged marriages. Marriages had implications for the whole extended family. Adultery was, therefore, far from a private matter. It affected everybody. It is indicative of its importance that Emperor Augustus issued a decree, the Lex Julia in 18 BCE, not only proscribing adultery but requiring that any man whose wife had committed adultery and had not taken her to court should himself be prosecuted. Philo of Alexandria, the Jewish philosopher and teacher writing in the mid-first century CE, even makes adultery the foremost of sins and cites as additional support for this claim the fact that in his Greek version of the two tablets of the ten commandments, unlike in most Hebrew texts, the prohibition of adultery comes first on the second table (*Decalogue* 121).

Israel's law had required execution of adulterers (Leviticus 20:10; Deuteronomy 22:22) but when Judea lost the right to inflict capital punishment under the Romans, the marriage had to be dissolved, as in Roman and Greek law. Divorce was mandatory, not an option. When Matthew cites Jesus' prohibition of divorce, he notes adultery as the exception (5:32; 19:9). For divorce always had to follow adultery. Matthew also depicts Jesus as declaring that not just the act but also the adulterous attitude and intent are to be avoided (5:28).

Make Wisdom Your Lover!

The image of the seductive woman in the hands of the author of Proverbs became more than just a warning to men about women who might seduce them into adultery. On the one hand, it came to symbolize sin and foolishness generally, depicted as the foolish woman or Woman Folly; and, on the other, it came to serve as a contrast to Wisdom, also depicted as a woman with whom men should form a relationship, Woman Wisdom.

We see the two Women contrasted in Proverbs 9. First, we have a depiction of Woman Wisdom:

> Wisdom has built her house, she has hewn her seven pillars. [2]She has slaughtered her animals, she has mixed her wine, she has also set her table. [3]She has sent out her servant-girls, she calls from the highest places in the town, [4]"You that are simple, turn in here!" To those without sense she says, [5]"Come, eat of my bread and drink of the wine I have mixed. [6]Lay aside immaturity, and live, and walk in the way of insight." (Proverbs 9:1–6)

Her behavior is patterned on her opposite, namely Woman Folly, who masquerades as a prostitute, inviting men to taste her wares.

Accordingly, the depiction of Woman Folly follows later in the chapter.

> The foolish woman is loud; she is ignorant and knows nothing. [14]She sits at the door of her house, on a seat at the high places of the town, [15]calling to those who pass by, who are going straight on their way, [16]"You who are simple, turn in here!" And to those without sense she says, [17]"Stolen water is sweet, and bread eaten in secret is pleasant." [18]But they do not know that the dead are there, that her guests are in the depths of Sheol. (Proverbs 9:13–18)

The words of invitation are the same, as is the behavior, but the consequences are diametrically opposite. While elements of sexual wrongdoing are still present, the image is now much larger than that of the individual adulteress. This was not lost on the translator of Proverbs into Greek, who regularly transposes what were originally warnings about sexual immorality into broader warnings about folly and sin.

Most remarkable is the creation of the image of Woman Wisdom based on the seductive immoral woman. We find it already in the first chapter: "Wisdom cries out in the street, in the squares she raises her voice. At the busiest corner she cries out; at the entrance of the city gates she speaks" (1:20–21). She is acting like a prostitute. She makes a reappearance in person in 8:4–36, similarly described as raising her voice at the crossroads and city gates.

> Does not wisdom call, and does not understanding raise her voice? [2]On the heights, beside the way, at the crossroads she takes her stand; [3]beside the gates in front of the town, at the entrance of the portals she cries out: [4]"To you, O people, I call, and my cry is to all

that live. ⁵O simple ones, learn prudence; acquire intelligence, you who lack it. ⁶Hear, for I will speak noble things, and from my lips will come what is right; ⁷for my mouth will utter truth; wickedness is an abomination to my lips." (Proverbs 8:1–7).

Wisdom represents God's law, as expounded by the author:

My child, keep my words and store up my commandments with you; ²keep my commandments and live, keep my teachings as the apple of your eye; ³bind them on your fingers, write them on the tablet of your heart. ⁴Say to wisdom, "You are my sister," and call insight your intimate friend, ⁵that they may keep you from the loose woman, from the adulteress with her smooth words. (Proverbs 7:1–5)

More strikingly, the author goes on to have Wisdom speak in person:

The LORD created me at the beginning of his work, the first of his acts of long ago. ²³Ages ago I was set up, at the first, before the beginning of the earth . . .²⁵Before the mountains had been shaped, before the hills, I was brought forth . . .²⁷When he established the heavens, I was there . . . when he marked out the foundations of the earth, ³⁰then I was beside him, like a master worker; and I was daily his delight, rejoicing before him always, ³¹rejoicing in his inhabited world and delighting in the human race. (Proverbs 8:22–23, 25, 27, 30–31)

This is an extraordinary development of the imagery. One way of reading it is to see it making the claim that God is all-wise and always has been from the beginning and saying so with poetic creativity which pictures God as having Woman Wisdom as a companion. The fact that in surrounding cultures there were goddesses of wisdom might have stimulated such thought. The words do not, however, depict Wisdom as simply eternal and part of God's character, but speak of it/her as something/someone created or brought to birth by God. This inevitably led to the notion that Wisdom was both God's own wisdom and also at the same time a separate being like an angel and so the myth of Wisdom Sophia (the Greek word for Wisdom) developed.

The author of Proverbs' flair for creativity as educating sage thus took the image of the seductive woman and transformed it into the contrasting image of Woman Wisdom issuing her own invitation of intimacy for the wise. Here it is noteworthy that the author does not depict Wisdom as mother of the wise, but rather as the partner and companion, indeed, their lover.

Others had written of Wisdom as a separate entity, such as we find in Job 28:

> But where shall wisdom be found? And where is the place of understanding? [13]Mortals do not know the way to it, and it is not found in the land of the living. . . . [20]Where then does wisdom come from? And where is the place of understanding? [21]It is hidden from the eyes of all living, and concealed from the birds of the air. [22]Abaddon and Death say, "We have heard a rumor of it with our ears." . . . [23]God understands the way to it, and he knows its place. . . . [28]And he said to humankind, "Truly, the fear of the Lord, that is wisdom; and to depart from evil is understanding." (Job 28:12–13, 20–23, 28)

The author of Proverbs went much further than the author of Job and thus stimulated the imagination of those who followed him. There are two main elements in his exposition. The first is that Woman Wisdom is the source of instruction, including the commandments. The second is that Wisdom had a hand in creation. Both lines of thought stimulated reflection and are always deeply connected. Indeed, the depiction of Wisdom as God's darling and companion has direct relevance for the author's moral instructions, limited as they are to how men should behave. For the implicit claim being made is that these instructions go back to how God made the world to be and especially how their world of households should be.

Consorting with Wisdom

The translator of Proverbs into Greek retains the imagery of Woman Wisdom while at times toning it down. The depiction of Wisdom in Proverbs 1:20–21 as crying out in the street, raising her voice, crying out on the corner of the top of the walls, and speaking at the city gates, a counter model to the seductress, is rendered less explicit. Instead, the Greek rewrites the image so that she "sings hymns in the streets," "leads frankly" in the squares, "proclaims on the top of the walls," "waits at the gates of the powerful," and "speaks boldly at the gates of the city." The image's origin in the street woman becomes less visible. Similarly, in 8:4 "she cries out" becomes "she sings hymns." In 7:4 "Say to Wisdom, 'You are my sister'" (7:4) becomes "Say that Wisdom is you sister."

For all the translator's hesitancy about the image's origin there is none in translating the depiction of Wisdom as God's companion in creation in Proverbs 8:22–31 or of Woman Wisdom's invitation in 9:1–6. In the instructions which follow before the depiction of the counter figure, Woman Folly, the translator makes an addition in 9:10 to bring the message home more explicitly. Thus "The fear of the LORD is the beginning of wisdom, and the knowledge of the Holy One is insight" becomes "The beginning of wisdom is the fear of the LORD and counsel of the saints is understanding, for to know the Law is the sign of a sound mind."

Ben Sira

The shift from instruction, primarily for men behaving badly, to instruction more broadly as God's will for how things should be, to the law explicitly, is evident also in Ben Sira writing around 180 BCE. He reworks Proverbs within his own depiction of sound advice. His work is included in the Apocrypha and sometimes called Ecclesiasticus. As noted above, he retained concerns with men's bad behavior and extended it. He did not, however, take up the image of Woman Folly. By contrast, he imaginatively filled out the imagery of Woman Wisdom as the lover of the wise and as their lover.

Ben Sira is best preserved in its Greek version which brings the document in full, but the original Hebrews survives for much of it, so that, as in Proverbs, we can see similarities and differences in the two versions. As with Proverbs, the translator, Ben Sira's grandson, tends to tone down the erotic imagery, though not eliminating it entirely.

In the opening chapter, surviving only in the Greek translation, Ben Sira combines Job 28 and Proverbs 8: "Wisdom was created before all other things, and prudent understanding from eternity. ⁶The root of wisdom—to whom has it been revealed? Her subtleties—who knows them? ⁸There is but one who is wise, greatly to be feared, seated upon his throne—the Lord. ⁹It is he who created her" (Ben Sira 1:5–9). There is movement from wisdom as an abstract notion like prudence to Wisdom as a person, as like a resourceful spouse bringing goods into a household:

"To fear the Lord is the beginning of wisdom; she is created with the faithful in the womb. ¹⁵She made among human beings an eternal foundation, and among their descendants she will abide faithfully. ¹⁶To fear the Lord is fullness of wisdom; she inebriates mortals with her fruits; ¹⁷she fills their whole house with desirable goods, and their storehouses with her produce" (Ben Sira 1:14–17). In 4:11–19 we have Wisdom as a teacher who invites the obedient to dwell in her inner most chambers, revealing to them her secret place, probably already with erotic connotations. The grandson's translation replaces "dwell in my innermost chambers" by "dwell in confidence" (4:15) and "reveal to him my secret place" by "reveal to him her secrets" (4:18). In 6:18–31 grandson retains the erotic imagery of sexual intercourse as ploughing and sowing in 6:19 and holding onto Wisdom and not letting her go (6:27) and being fettered in bondage by her (6:24–25) and yoked to her (6:30), images of seduction and marriage.

Erotic imagery continues in 14:12—15:10, especially in 14:23–26, which speaks of peeping through Woman Wisdom's window, listening at her doors, encamping by her house, driving one's tent peg into her wall (sexual penetration), putting one's tent by her side, and in 15:2–3 being met by her as a young bride, who also offers bread and water. The grandson tones down "who builds his nest in her foliage and in her branches spends the night" in 14:26 to read "who places his children under her shelter, and lodges under her boughs."

Erotic imagery continues in 51:13–30 and, again, is toned down by the grandson. Thus, "I was young and before I went astray, I kept seeking her" (51:13) becomes "When I was still young, before I wandered, I sought wisdom plainly in my prayers." "She came to me in her beauty" (51:14) becomes "before the temple I asked for her." "I planned to make sport. I was zealous for pleasure and did not cease" (51:18) becomes "I resolved to do it (i.e., wisdom)." In 51:19–20 the author refers to exaltation, to the hand and to opening wisdom's gate, allusions to orgasm and sexual penetration. The grandson simply refers to hands lifted to heaven in prayer. The reference in 51:21, 23 to the fire of sexual passion and the invitation to spend with night with Wisdom become an invitation to lodge in the place of learning.

As with Proverbs, the more "respectable" translation does not detract from the emphasis on Wisdom in personal terms representing God's law. This is especially evident in 24:1–22 where Ben Sira reworks Proverbs 8. Here, too, Wisdom speaks of her role at the beginning of time. "Wisdom praises herself, and tells of her glory in the midst of her people. ²In the assembly of the Most High she opens her mouth, and in the presence of his hosts she tells of her glory: ³I came forth from the mouth of the Most High, and covered the earth like a mist. ⁴I dwelt in the highest heavens, and my throne was in a pillar of cloud'" (Ben Sira 24:1–4). The allusions to the

Spirit moving over the waters at creation in Genesis 1:2 and to God's presence in the pillar of cloud during the Exodus are unmistakable. Even more significant is the report of Wisdom's seeking a place to dwell: "Among all these I sought a resting-place; in whose territory should I abide? [8]Then the Creator of all things gave me a command, and my Creator chose the place for my tent. He said, 'Make your dwelling in Jacob, and in Israel receive your inheritance'" (Ben Sira 24:7–8).

Ben Sira celebrates that Wisdom, God's companion at creation, found a dwelling place in Zion: "Before the ages, in the beginning, he created me, and for all the ages I shall not cease to be. [10]In the holy tent I ministered before him, and so I was established in Zion. [11]Thus in the beloved city he gave me a resting-place, and in Jerusalem was my domain. [12]I took root in an honored people, in the portion of the Lord, his heritage" (Ben Sira 24:9–12). Wisdom thus issues its invitation, echoing her call in Proverbs 9: "Come to me, you who desire me, and eat your fill of my fruits. [20]For the memory of me is sweeter than honey, and the possession of me sweeter than the honeycomb. [21]Those who eat of me will hunger for more, and those who drink of me will thirst for more" (Ben Sira 24:19–21). As in the Greek translator's addition to Proverbs 9:10, so Ben Sira makes very clear: "All this is the book of the covenant of the Most High God, the law that Moses commanded us as an inheritance for the congregations of Jacob" (24:23). From instruction to men behaving badly to instruction to do God's will, Wisdom now represents and is identified with the law and hailed as a source of nourishment for those who hunger and thirst.

Ben Sira concludes his work with Wisdom's invitation: "Draw near to me, you who are uneducated, and lodge in the house of instruction. [24]Why do you say you are lacking in these things, and why do you endure such great thirst? [25]I opened my mouth and said, Acquire wisdom for yourselves without money. [26]Put your neck under her yoke, and let your souls receive instruction; it is to be found close by" (Ben Sira 51:23–26). It finds its echo in the invitation of Jesus in Matthew: "Come to me, all you that are weary and are carrying heavy burdens, and I will give you rest. [29]Take my yoke upon you, and learn from me; for I am gentle and humble in heart, and you will find rest for your souls. [30]For my yoke is easy, and my burden is light" (Matthew 11:28–30).

Baruch

Ben Sira's direct equation of Woman Wisdom with the law is briefly paralleled in the book of Baruch, written about the same time and also included in the Apocrypha, In its hymn to Wisdom it also plays with imagery from Job 28 and Proverbs 8. "Learn where there is wisdom, where there is strength, where there is understanding, so that you may at the same time discern where there is length of days, and life, where there is light for the eyes, and peace. ¹⁵Who has found her place? And who has entered her storehouses?" (Baruch 3:14–15). As in Job 28, Baruch declares that God alone knows Wisdom: "Who has gone up into heaven, and taken her, and brought her down from the clouds? ³⁰Who has gone over the sea, and found her, and will buy her for pure gold? ³¹No one knows the way to her, or is concerned about the path to her. ³²But the one who knows all things knows her, he found her by his understanding" (Baruch 3:29–32). As in Ben Sira 24 the author then acclaims her descent to dwell in Israel: "This is our God; no other can be compared to him. ³⁶He found the whole way to knowledge, and gave her to his servant Jacob and to Israel, whom he loved. ³⁷Afterwards she appeared on earth and lived with humankind" (Baruch 3:35–37).

He goes on, similarly, to identify her with the law: "She is the book of the commandments of God, the law that endures for ever. All who hold her fast will live, and those who forsake her will die. ²Turn, O Jacob, and take her; walk towards the shining of her light" (Baruch 4:1–2).

Wisdom, the law, is thus food and drink, light and life.

The Parables of Enoch

The notion of Wisdom as descending to issue an invitation to humankind finds a parallel in the Parables of Enoch (first century CE), incorporated in the collection known as the book of 1 Enoch, which we visited in our discussion of the myth of the watchers. There in 1 Enoch 42 we read a much less optimistic account of Wisdom's coming to Israel, for it depicts Israel as rejecting her offer: "Wisdom did not find a place where she might dwell. So her dwelling was in the heaven. Wisdom went forth to dwell among the sons of men, but she did not find a dwelling. Wisdom returned to her place, and sat down among the angels. Iniquity went forth from her chambers. Those whom she did not seek she found, and she dwelt among them like rain in a desert and dew in a thirsty land" (1 Enoch 42:1–2).

Here the author sets "Iniquity" in contrast to Wisdom as Proverbs had done with Woman Folly.

Wisdom of Solomon

The Wisdom of Solomon, now found in the Apocrypha of the Christian Bible, was composed in Greek in the mid-first century CE probably in Alexandria and attributed in honor to Solomon who lived almost a millennium earlier. It also picks up the theme of Wisdom, but with fewer erotic traits and with more emphasis on Wisdom's intimate connection with God at creation and ever since. It is written in sophisticated Greek style and there are signs that the author was well versed in Hellenistic culture, including streams of Middle Platonism and Stoicism.

It, too, speaks of Wisdom in personal terms. Thus, it begins: "Love righteousness, you rulers of the earth, think of the Lord in goodness and seek him with sincerity of heart; [2]because he is found by those who do not put him to the test, and manifests himself to those who do not distrust him. [3]For perverse thoughts separate people from God, and when his power is tested, it exposes the foolish; [4]because wisdom will not enter a deceitful soul, or dwell in a body enslaved to sin" (Wisdom 1:1–4). The author has Solomon issue warnings against a range of sins, not specifically sexual, and offer an accolade to Wisdom that expands the tradition identified in Proverbs, Ben Sira, and Baruch. It begins: "Wisdom is radiant and unfading, and she is easily discerned by those who love her, and is found by those who seek her. [13]She hastens to make herself known to those who desire her. [14]One who rises early to seek her will have no difficulty, for she will be found sitting at the gate" (Wisdom 6:12–14). It goes on to say that "Wisdom goes about seeking those worthy of her, and she graciously appears to them in their paths, and meets them in every thought" (6:16) and to assert her connection with the law: "love of her is the keeping of her laws, and giving heed to her laws is assurance of immortality" (6:18). "Solomon" thus claims: "wisdom, the fashioner of all things, taught me" (7:22).

The author acclaims her qualities:

> There is in her a spirit that is intelligent, holy, unique, manifold, subtle, mobile, clear, unpolluted, distinct, invulnerable, loving the good, keen, irresistible, [23]beneficent, humane, steadfast, sure, free from anxiety, all-powerful, overseeing all, and penetrating through all spirits that are intelligent, pure, and altogether subtle. [24]For

wisdom is more mobile than any motion; because of her pureness
she pervades and penetrates all things. (Wisdom 7:22–24)

These qualities go beyond simple goodness to identify qualities of life
widely affirmed among Hellenistic philosophers of the author's world and
coherent also with his Jewish faith.

He then reflects on Wisdom's relationship to God:

> For she is a breath of the power of God, and a pure emanation
> of the glory of the Almighty; therefore nothing defiled gains
> entrance into her. 26For she is a reflection of eternal light, a spot-
> less mirror of the working of God, and an image of his good-
> ness. 27Although she is but one, she can do all things, and while
> remaining in herself, she renews all things; in every generation
> she passes into holy souls and makes them friends of God, and
> prophets; 28for God loves nothing so much as the person who
> lives with wisdom. (Wisdom 7:25–28)

In this way the author goes beyond both Proverbs and Ben Sira to depict
Wisdom as being an emanation of God's glory, the image, mirror, and reflection of God, and as active throughout creation and entering people. Her
role in relation to "all things" would recall for those versed in popular Stoic
philosophy the notion of the Logos seen as a divine force penetrating all
reality and giving it order. The notion of such order fitted in well in Jewish
thought with the notion of God's law, so that they could speak of Wisdom
also in such terms as being the Logos, the word upholding all things, and
engaged with people. As 8:1 puts it, "She reaches mightily from one end of
the earth to the other, and she orders all things well."

The marital imagery in relation to Woman Wisdom, both in relation
to Solomon and to God, returns strongly in chapter 8, where the author has
Solomon declare: "I loved her and sought her from my youth; I desired to
take her for my bride, and became enamored of her beauty. 3She glorifies
her noble birth by living with God, and the Lord of all loves her. 4For she
is an initiate in the knowledge of God, and an associate in his works" (Wis
8:2–4). Solomon reports his prayer to God that he might have her:

> O God of my ancestors and Lord of mercy, who have made all
> things by your word, 2and by your wisdom have formed human-
> kind to have dominion over the creatures you have made, 3and
> rule the world in holiness and righteousness, and pronounce
> judgement in uprightness of soul, 4give me the wisdom that sits

by your throne, and do not reject me from among your servants. (Wisdom 9:1–4)

Here we see "word" and "wisdom" set in parallel, but still within a context which imagines Wisdom as sitting beside God's throne.

Solomon continues: "With you is wisdom, she who knows your works and was present when you made the world; she understands what is pleasing in your sight and what is right according to your commandments. [10]Send her forth from the holy heavens, and from the throne of your glory send her, that she may labor at my side, and that I may learn what is pleasing to you. [11]For she knows and understands all things, and she will guide me wisely in my actions and guard me with her glory" (Wisdom 9:9–11).

The writing continues over the following chapters with an account of how Wisdom was active at creation and throughout history from Adam onwards.

Philo of Alexandria

Also active in the first century CE in Alexandria was Philo, the Jewish philosopher, similarly well versed in the Hellenistic philosophy of his time and author of multiple works which have survived. He frequently employs the image of the seductress. Its biblical roots reach back into Proverbs 1–9, but he knows it as a standard illustration in philosophy in the form preserved in Xenophon *Memorabilia* 2.1, which depicts two women of contrasting character. For Philo one is Pleasure, depicted as seductive, characterized by "villainy, recklessness, faithlessness, flattery, imposture, deceit, falsehood, perjury, impiety, injustice, profligacy" (*Sacrifices* 22) and representing wickedness in general. The other Philo praises for "her loveliness, so pure, so simple, so holy to look upon" (*Sacrifices* 45) and provides an extensive list of her virtues. Her message, like that of woman Wisdom in Proverbs, is to warn of the dangers of the other woman, but here without particular focus on sexual wrongdoing.

More significantly, Philo speaks of Wisdom's relationship to God. Reflecting the hierarchy of gender values of his time he writes: "That which comes after God, even though it were chiefest of all things, occupies a second place, and therefore was termed feminine to express its contrast with the Maker of the Universe who is masculine, and its affinity to everything else" (*Flight* 51). His preference, however, is to reinterpret the image of Woman Wisdom and not be bound to gender categories. To this end he writes: "Let us, then, pay no heed to the discrepancy in the gender of the words, and say that the daughter of God, even Wisdom, is not only masculine but father, sowing and begetting in souls aptness to learn, discipline, knowledge, sound sense, good and laudable actions" (*Flight* 52).

Philo's preference was to speak of God's Logos (word), a term which he was able to connect to the Stoic notion of Logos penetrating all things. However, for him, rather than being an impersonal reality, Logos had personal character as God's Wisdom or word. Therefore, unlike Ben Sirah 24, he speaks not of Wisdom but of Logos, the word, descending (*Dreams* 1.85–86). On the relation between (Wisdom) Logos and God, Philo can speak of the Logos as God's firstborn son (*Agriculture* 51; *Confusion* 146) or even as "god" (*Dreams* 1.229–30) or as a "second god" (*Questions and Answers on Genesis* 2.62), reflecting the flexible use of such designations we found in discussing royal ideology in the previous chapter and so without in any sense intending to say there is more than one God. Nor does Philo use the imagery of seduction to depict Wisdom or the Logos.

We see then a development from what in part is a clever educational ploy on the part of the teacher who wrote Proverbs 1–9, calling wayward men to fall in love with Woman Wisdom, to seeing Woman Wisdom as embodying God's law and as God's companion in creation and as engaged in human history, and finally to the merging of Wisdom and Logos imagery most fully present in Philo. In Alexandria and elsewhere where Jews lived and worked in the context of Hellenistic culture it was to some extent to be expected that what began and developed as a way of talking of God's law became a way of talking about how to live in the wider world in harmony with the order of divine creation. What began on the margins in moral instruction became then a vehicle for understanding the heart of reality. It moved to the center.

Finding Wisdom in the Jesus Story

Woman Wisdom seemingly makes no appearance in the story of Jesus. As we found in discussing the term "Messiah" in the previous chapter, Wisdom, too, barely gains a mention in the sayings of Jesus in contrast to "kingdom of God" and "Son of Man." It is marginal. There are just a few references, and they are to be found in one of our earliest sources which lay behind Matthew and Luke, upon which they drew and which they adapted to their purpose in their broader narrative. It is commonly identified by the first letter of the German word for source, "Quelle," and so called "Q." Luke tended to stay closer to the earlier form of the sayings whereas Matthew or perhaps people before him polished the sayings somewhat to produce a better outcome rhetorically and also theologically.

Our most direct example is to be found in Luke among Jesus' challenges to the Pharisees. The same material appears in Matt 23 in reworked form. Here is Luke's version, which portrays Jesus' response to one of their specialist interpreters, somewhat anachronistically translated as "lawyers":

> Woe to you! For you build the tombs of the prophets whom your ancestors killed. [48]So you are witnesses and approve of the deeds of your ancestors; for they killed them, and you build their tombs. [49]Therefore also the Wisdom of God said, "I will send them prophets and apostles, some of whom they will kill and persecute," [50]so that this generation may be charged with the blood of all the prophets shed since the foundation of the world, [51]from the blood of Abel to the blood of Zechariah, who perished between the altar and the sanctuary. Yes, I tell you, it will be charged against this generation. (Luke 11:47–51)

The response has Jesus cite Woman Wisdom. It may be having Jesus quote directly from an unknown source or simply having him cite in summary what Wisdom had always been saying. In substance, it portrays Wisdom as one who sent prophets and apostles. The reference to apostles may indicate that the saying comes not from the time of Jesus but from the time of the early church, so that both this saying of Wisdom and the saying attributed to Jesus which includes it are products of what the early church sensed Jesus would have said in the context of their escalating conflicts with fellow Jews.

The term "apostle" means "sent one" and reflects the nature of telecommunication in the world of the time. There was, of course, no postal service, let alone telephone or internet service. People did write letters and would often send someone to deliver then who would need to be authenticated. This was usually about much more than being the deliverer. It often meant that the one sent, usually a man, had to operate on behalf of the one sending him. Thus, a sent one or envoy carried the authority of the sender and could often speak and act on the sender's behalf. In the saying above, Wisdom is the sender and the prophets and apostles are understood to have been authorized at least to convey Wisdom's message and in that sense act on Wisdom's behalf.

One of the other sayings which mentions Wisdom depicts John the Baptist and Jesus as envoys of Wisdom: "To what then will I compare the people of this generation, and what are they like? [32]They are like children sitting in the marketplace and calling to one another, "We played the flute for you, and you did not dance; we wailed, and you did not weep." [33]For John the Baptist has come eating no bread and drinking no wine, and you say, "He has a demon"; [34]the Son of Man has come eating and drinking, and you say, "Look, a glutton and a drunkard, a friend of tax-collectors and sinners!" [35]Nevertheless, wisdom is vindicated by all her children" (Luke 7:31–35). Here John and Jesus are portrayed as children of Wisdom.

The author of Matthew's Gospel has revised these sayings, changing them in significant ways. His version of the contrast between John and Jesus is substantially the same as in Luke except for the final statement, where "Nevertheless, wisdom is vindicated by all her children," almost certainly the earlier form of the saying, becomes "Yet wisdom is vindicated by her deeds" (11:19). John and Jesus are not children of Wisdom, although they do Wisdom's deeds.

The change is even more striking in Matthew's version of the passage above which depicts Jesus citing Wisdom. Matthew's version has Jesus, himself, declare:

> Therefore I send you prophets, sages, and scribes, some of whom you will kill and crucify, and some you will flog in your synagogues and pursue from town to town, [35]so that upon you may come all the righteous blood shed on earth, from the blood of righteous Abel to the blood of Zechariah son of Barachiah, whom you murdered between the sanctuary and the altar. [36]Truly I tell you, all this will come upon this generation. (Matthew 23:34–36)

Here Matthew's Jesus speaks with the voice of Wisdom. Two further sayings also depict Jesus speaking in this way. One follows directly in Matthew on the saying just cited:

> Jerusalem, Jerusalem, the city that kills the prophets and stones those who are sent to it! How often have I desired to gather your children together as a hen gathers her brood under her wings, and you were not willing! [38]See, your house is left to you, desolate. [39]For I tell you, you will not see me again until you say, "Blessed is the one who comes in the name of the Lord." (Matthew 23:37–39)

This is an image of Wisdom as a mother hen depicting Wisdom's envoys across Israel's history now voiced by Jesus as his own words. It is also to be found on Luke 13:34–35 in virtually identical form. The second saying is to be found only in Matthew: "Come to me, all you that are weary and are carrying heavy burdens, and I will give you rest. [29]Take my yoke upon you, and learn from me; for I am gentle and humble in heart, and you will find rest for your souls. [30]For my yoke is easy, and my burden is light" (Matthew 11:28–30). As we saw in discussing Ben Sira, this saying echoes how that work ends, where Ben Sira appeals to people to take upon themselves the yoke of the Law (51:23–26). A distinctive feature of Matthew's Gospel is that the author presents Jesus as the advocate of the law and its true interpreter in contrast to those who apply it ways that bind heavy burdens on people. As 23:4 puts it: "They tie up heavy burdens, hard to bear, and lay them on the shoulders of others; but they themselves are unwilling to lift a finger to move them." The Sermon on the Mount has Jesus make his stance very clear:

"Do not think that I have come to abolish the law or the prophets; I have come not to abolish but to fulfill. [18]For truly I tell you, until heaven and earth pass away, not one letter, not one stroke of a letter, will pass from the law until all is accomplished. [19]Therefore, whoever breaks one of the least of these commandments, and teaches others to do the same, will be called least in the kingdom of heaven; but whoever does them and teaches them will be called great in the kingdom of heaven" (Matthew 5:17–19). In that sense Matthew stands on continuity with Ben Sira and Baruch in identifying Wisdom and God's law and goes beyond them in claiming Jesus as the mouthpiece of Wisdom or perhaps even more, as Wisdom itself. We can say this on the basis, however, of very few texts, so that one can hardly make the claim that it was central to the author's or to Jesus' concerns, who expressed himself in different terms like kingdom of God and Son of Man. At most one might say that in Matthew Jesus as Son of Man will be the judge to come, announced by John, and so be the one who will apply the law.

Wisdom and Royal Messianic Streams

The Gospel according to Mark, written earlier than Matthew and Luke and used by them as a source, has no sayings or reflections which use the image of Woman Wisdom or ideas connected with it. By contrast, the Gospel according to John abounds with such allusions. Before, however, we turn to that Gospel, it is instructive to trace another development which took place well before it was written. It relates to a problem we noted in the previous chapter, namely the problem of using royal messianic language beyond those Jewish contexts where hope for a Messiah was a national focus for many. Were there other ways of depicting Jesus' risen status which were not dependent on such language which seemed so much tied up with Jewish national identity? Indeed, there were, and here we find that the myth of Woman Wisdom and the ideas associated with it provided a significant bridge and so moved from the margins to the very center of faith.

The best example of the meeting of both streams, the royal messianic and the Wisdom streams, is found in Hebrews 1. As we saw in the previous chapter, there are clear traces there of the myth of divine kingship. I enclose the source of the relevant allusions and quotations in brackets.

> He sat down at the right hand of the Majesty on high [Psalm 110:1], ⁴having become as much superior to angels as the name he has inherited is more excellent than theirs. ⁵For to which of the angels did God ever say, "You are my Son; today I have begotten you" [Psalm 2:7]? Or again, "I will be his Father, and he will be my Son" [2 Samuel 7:14]? ⁶And again, when he brings the firstborn [Psalm 89:27] into the world, he says, "Let all God's angels worship him." . . . But of the Son he says, "Your throne, O God, is for ever and ever, and the righteous scepter is the scepter of your kingdom. ⁹You have loved righteousness and hated wickedness; therefore God, your God, has anointed you with the oil of gladness beyond your companions" [Psalm 45:6–7]. (Hebrews 1:3–9)

It is a veritable assembly of allusions and quotations relating to the enthronement of Israel's kings, given the name and status of being Son of God, now applied to Jesus' resurrection and exaltation. On either side of this block of material are other statements which clearly reflect the myth of Woman Wisdom which has now been reconfigured to describe Jesus: "Long ago God spoke to our ancestors in many and various ways by the prophets, ²but in these last days he has spoken to us by a Son, whom he appointed heir of all things, through whom he also created the worlds. ³He is the reflection of God's glory and the exact imprint of God's very being, and he sustains all things by his powerful word" (Hebrews 1:1–3). Jesus, like Wisdom, was God's aid in creation and sustaining it. On the other side of the royal messianic imagery the Wisdom imagery returns. The author cites a Psalm about God and applies it to Jesus as part of the proof of his superiority to angels: "And, "In the beginning, Lord, you founded the earth, and the heavens are the work of your hands; ¹¹they will perish, but you remain; they will all wear out like clothing; [12]like a cloak you will roll them up, and like clothing they will be changed. But you are the same, and your years will never end" (Hebrews 1:10–12).

The Wisdom stream had depicted Wisdom as active in creation and in sustaining the creation and as being a reflection and mirror of God, God's child, also able to be called "God." Now such terms are being applied to Jesus. We can imagine the process. People acclaimed that by raising Jesus from the dead God had enthroned him as Messiah and Son of God, not just to come, but also as ruling beside God. They realized that there was another way of describing this role. It was to pick up the image of Wisdom which also described the one through whom God ruled and could also be called "Son of God" and be spoken of in masculine terms. The shift from the female image of Wisdom to the masculine or more neutral image of the power under God as God's Word or Logos had already been made in such authors as Philo and probably elsewhere as well. Accordingly, they proclaimed that Jesus now holds the position in heaven which had been held by Wisdom/Logos.

More than that, Jesus is God's Word, God's Wisdom, second in charge. To speak of Jesus as the power, the Logos, by which God ruled not just Israel but the whole creation, made much more sense to people outside of Israel than to talk of him as the Jewish Messiah (the Christ). It also made sense for those Jews living within the wider world.

This acclamation of Jesus in the language and imagery which had its origin in the myth of Woman Wisdom opened new possibilities for thought and reflection. Whereas notions of royal messiahship were largely limited to depicting Jesus' status since his resurrection and before that as Messiah designate, notions of Jesus as the Wisdom/Logos power under God went far beyond that. Accordingly, as Wisdom/Logos was with God from the beginning, active in creation and in Israel's history, God's agent and God's Son, so faith could affirm that Jesus not only lived beyond the grave by resurrection, but lived before his birth as Wisdom/Logos, God's Son, and as such was the one through whom God created all things.

This explains how the author of Hebrews can speak of him as God's "Son, whom he appointed heir of all things, through whom he also created the worlds. [3]He is the reflection of God's glory and the exact imprint of God's very being, and he sustains all things by his powerful word" (1:2–3). He was and is doing, according to the author, exactly what the Wisdom/Logos stream had acclaimed of Wisdom. His language also echoes the language of the Book of Wisdom which spoke of Wisdom as "a breath of the power of God, and a pure emanation of the glory of the Almighty; therefore nothing defiled gains entrance into her. [26]For she is a reflection of eternal light, a spotless mirror of the working of God, and an image of his goodness" (Wisdom 7:25–26).

The author of Hebrews merges both streams, royal messianic and Wisdom, into his statement about the Son's status as superior to the angels and so uses "Son" in two different senses. "Son" is the throne name he receives at his resurrection and enthronement according to the royal messianic stream (1:4), but he was also the divine Son long before that, from creation (1:2). We must assume that the author saw no contradiction in this and was aware that he was using two different frames of reference, royal messianic and wisdom.

We find a similar juxtaposition of statements and streams of thought In Colossians, also about Jesus' resurrection and his role in creation like Wisdom. Colossians was written probably by an admirer of Paul and seeks to represent his views in a new situation where some had fears about angels and powers and how faith should see them. It begins by acclaiming Jesus using the Wisdom stream: "He is the image of the invisible God, the firstborn of all creation; [16]for in him all things in heaven and on earth were created, things visible and invisible, whether thrones or dominions or rulers or powers—all things have been created through him and for him. [17]He himself is before all things, and in him all things hold together" (Colossians 1:15–17).

It then goes on to describe the significance of his resurrection: "He is the head of the body, the church; he is the beginning, the firstborn from the dead, so that he might come to have first place in everything. [19]For in him all the fullness of God was pleased to dwell, [20]and through him God was pleased to reconcile to himself all things, whether on earth or in heaven, by making peace through the blood of his cross" (Colossians 1:18–20). He is firstborn in two senses, as in Hebrews he is Son in two senses: "firstborn of all creation" and "firstborn from the dead." The statements have a poetic ring which has led some to suggest that it may be citing a hymn. It is certainly reflecting use of the wisdom stream, but one can see how it also incorporates not only resurrection but also Jesus' earthly ministry.

The two different uses of "Son" can be found also in the beginning of Paul's letter to the Romans, where he appears to be establishing common ground with them by citing a tradition about the gospel which he knew they would join him in affirming. He writes, "the gospel concerning his Son, who was descended from David according to the flesh ⁴and was declared to be Son of God with power according to the spirit of holiness by resurrection from the dead, Jesus Christ our Lord" (Romans 1:3–4). The first use of "Son" matches Paul's use elsewhere, where he speaks of God sending his Son, such as later in 8:3, where he writes of God "sending his own Son in the likeness of sinful flesh" and in 8:32, that God "did not withhold his own Son, but gave him up for all of us." "Son" refers to the whole of Jesus' life. By contrast, "Son of God" in Paul's words, literally "appointed Son of God with power according to the Spirit of holiness from his resurrection from the dead," employs the royal messianic stream of thought according to which at his resurrection Jesus, appropriately qualified as belonging to the seed of David, was enthroned and given the name and so the status of being "Son of God" as God's Messiah. Paul may be reflecting sensitivity to the two different usages when he adds the words "with power."

Elsewhere, Paul appears to employ Wisdom tradition when he writes of: "one Lord, Jesus Christ, through whom are all things and through whom we exist" (1 Corinthians 8:6), alluding to his role in creation. He appears also to draw on diverse traditions in speaking of Jesus' origins. They include that Jesus the Son was sent as prophets were sent. In Philippians there is another poetic-sounding piece, perhaps a tradition, in which Paul cites the example of Jesus: "Christ Jesus, ⁶who, though he was in the form of God, did not regard equality with God as something to be exploited, ⁷but emptied himself, taking the form of a slave, being born in human likeness. And being found in human form, ⁸he humbled himself and became obedient to the point of death—even death on a cross" (Philippians 2:5–8). It, too, may be reflecting the impact of the Wisdom stream, if being in the form of God reflects the notion of Wisdom as God's image. The poetic piece continues with a reference to Jesus' exaltation and receiving God's name: "Therefore God also highly exalted him and gave him the name that is above every name, ¹⁰so that at the name of Jesus every knee should bend, in heaven and on earth and under the earth, ¹¹and every tongue should confess that Jesus Christ is Lord, to the glory of God the Father" (Philippians 2:9–11).

The "name" here is not "Son" but God's own name, "Lord," but the scenery is certainly that of a royal court with all present kneeling in adoration.

From the Margins to the Middle:
Wisdom/Logos in John

The stream which flowed through the myth of Woman Wisdom is most evident in the Gospel according to John. We encounter it in the opening chapter: "In the beginning was the Word, and the Word was with God, and the Word was God. [2]He was in the beginning with God. [3]All things came into being through him, and without him not one thing came into being" (John 1:1–3). As Wisdom/Logos was with God from the beginning and in its role could be called "God" and was active in creation, so the Logos, the Word, here identified with Jesus, is all these things. More than that, Jesus is Wisdom/Logos. As Wisdom/Logos was light and life, so Jesus the Word is light and life. As Ben Sira depicts the descent of Wisdom, so the John's Gospel speaks of Jesus the Word descending, but like 1 Enoch 42, the Word, Wisdom, finds almost no welcome: "The true light, which enlightens everyone, was coming into the world. [10]He was in the world, and the world came into being through him; yet the world did not know him. [11]He came to what was his own, and his own people did not accept him. [12]But to all who received him, who believed in his name, he gave power to become children of God, [13]who were born, not of blood or of the will of the flesh or of the will of man, but of God" (John 1:9–13).

The statements in John 1 about the Word, the Logos, like others we have encountered, have a poetic lilt and may therefore be something which the author is adapting for the introduction to his Gospel. Possibly in its earlier form it reported how the Word/Logos visited Israel through the prophets and that those who did respond positively were deemed to be born as God's children. This could even have been its meaning before Christ believers adapted it. Possibly the latter also saw it this way and then added as a climax the words, "And the Word became flesh and lived among us, and we have seen his glory, glory as of the only Son of the Father [NRSV has "glory as of a father's only son" which I consider not adequate for the context], full of grace and truth" (1:14). He came to Israel through the prophets and finally came in the flesh in Jesus.

In the hands of the author, however, the whole passage from 1:9–18 is about Jesus as the Word and his coming, so that when it speaks about his coming to his own in 1:9 and 11, it is referring already to Jesus' ministry. That would make sense of the reference already in 1:12 to those receiving him being born as God's children, an idea elsewhere preserved to describe a believing response to Jesus and his ministry. Then the reference to the Word becoming flesh in 1:14 was not for the author the detailing of a new event, but rather an elaboration of the significance of his coming, already announced in 1:9, namely how he came. That also makes good sense of the fact that the author makes reference in the immediately preceding verses to John the Baptist (1:6–8), as he does again in 1:15. This means also that already in 1:4–5 where the author speaks of the Word/Logos shining in the darkness he is referring to Jesus' earthly ministry and its significance: "What has come into being ⁴in him was life, and the life was the light of all people. ⁵The light shines in the darkness, and the darkness did not overcome it."

When we turn to the conclusion of these statements by the author in 1:14–18 about Jesus as the Word/Logos, we can see some distinctive tweaking in which the author has engaged. He begins with the extraordinary claim: "And the Word became flesh." There is no precedent for this in the Wisdom/Logos stream. It is to be accounted for by the fact that the author and many other Christ believers are identifying Jesus not just as in the stream as a bearer of Wisdom/Logos but as Wisdom/Logos himself, a conundrum which has baffled people ever since.

As the passage proceeds, we find elements typical of statements in the stream, literally: "and tented among us, and we have seen his glory, the glory as of only Son of the Father, full of grace and truth" (1:14). Wisdom according to Ben Sira had similarly chosen to take up her dwelling on earth, in Israel, and the Wisdom/Logos stream also depicted Wisdom/Logos as God's Son and as reflecting God's glory.

The return in 1:15 to John the Baptist helps reinforce the identity of Jesus with the Logos/Word and so as having been in existence before his ministry, for John declares: "He who comes after me ranks ahead of me because he was before me." The author joins the acclamation in declaring: "From his fullness we have all received, grace upon grace" (1:16). The literal translation is "grace instead of/in place of grace" and means one gift in place of another. The author quickly identifies these gifts in the next verse. They are gifts from God: "The law indeed was given through Moses; grace and truth came through Jesus Christ." Jesus, the Logos Word, is the greater gift which thus replaces the previous gift, the law. To underline this fact the author then declares: "No one has ever seen God. It is God the only Son, who is close to the Father's heart, who has made him known" (1:18). The implication is clear: only the Son, who alone has seen the Father, can make him known. Whatever other benefits the law had brought, this was something which only the Son, the Logos/Word could achieve.

This is a departure from the implicit and sometimes explicit identification of Wisdom with the law, such as we find directly in Ben Sira and Baruch and has profound implications for how we understand the rest of the Gospel. The author's introduction, sometimes called the prologue, sets the scene and establishes the basis on which what follows is to be understood. Its readers or hearers, many of whom would have been Jews, would therefore have been familiar with the stream of Wisdom/Logos and its imagery. Through Proverbs 8, Ben Sira, Baruch, the Wisdom of Solomon, they would have known that, identified with Wisdom, the law was also celebrated as light, life, water, bread, the way and the truth.

The author has reconfigured the stories of Jesus in his narrative in a way that, however they functioned in the past, they are now to be heard as testimonies to the fact that now Jesus, alone, is the light, life, water, bread, the way and the truth, not the law. He alone is the Logos, the Word, with God in the beginning, co-creator, and now the bringer of new life. This is an extraordinary turnaround. The author, following standard practice of the time, created speeches of Jesus, seeking to portray what he sensed was Jesus' message. Luke had done that in writing speeches for key figures in his history of the early church, but in John the artistic work is much more extensive and creative.

Jesus' encounter with a Samaritan woman becomes a message that Jesus offers living water, as had Wisdom to the thirsty in the Wisdom/Logos stream. He expanded the feeding of the five thousand with a discourse which frowned on those who treated it primarily as miracle and failed to see that its message was that Jesus is the bread of life and so has Jesus declare: "I am the bread of life. Whoever comes to me will never be hungry, and whoever believes in me will never be thirsty" (6:35).

Similarly, the healing of the blind becomes a platform for having Jesus declare, "I am the light of the world" (9:5), an image also inspired by the symbolism of the lighting of candles at the Feast of Tabernacles, echoing his declaration in 8:12, "I am the light of the world. Whoever follows me will never walk in darkness but will have the light of life."

In the same way, the author makes the raising of Lazarus the platform for having Jesus declare: "I am the resurrection and the life. Those who believe in me, even though they die, will live, [26]and everyone who lives and believes in me will never die" (11:25–26). In the extensive last discourses, which the author created following the model of biographies of the period of depicting the hero's famous last words of advice to their followers, he has Jesus declare, "I am the way, and the truth, and the life. No one comes to the Father except through me" (14:6) and "I am the true vine, and my Father is the vine-grower" (15:1); "I am the vine, you are the branches. Those who abide in me and I in them bear much fruit, because apart from me you can do nothing" (15:5).

In all of these images, the author is applying to Jesus what in the tradition had been applied to the Law as the embodiment of Wisdom/ Logos. Now Jesus is the embodiment of Wisdom/Logos. The implications of this creative development are far-reaching. For now, the good news is primarily that Wisdom/Logos has come in Jesus and that to find life one needs to enter a relationship with Jesus, the risen Jesus represented now by the Spirit. This eclipses what in much tradition had been the focus, namely forgiveness of sins and reconciliation with God on the basis of Jesus' death. The author retains that tradition, but it no longer takes center stage. What matters most is accepting the offer of relationship through Jesus the Word incarnate.

The author stops short of employing romantic, let alone erotic, attachment to describe this relationship in the way that Proverbs and especially Ben Sira do. The language remains, however, intimate, speaking of love and of abiding in the other. It coheres well with the image of the vine: "Abide in me as I abide in you. Just as the branch cannot bear fruit by itself unless it abides in the vine, neither can you unless you abide in me" (15:4), but is applied more generally as in Jesus' final prayer for his own:

> I ask not only on behalf of these, but also on behalf of those who will believe in me through their word, [21]that they may all be one. As you, Father, are in me and I am in you, may they also be in us, so that the world may believe that you have sent me. [22]The glory that you have given me I have given them, so that they may be one, as we are one, [23]I in them and you in me, that they may become completely one, so that the world may know that you have sent me and have loved them even as you have loved me. (John 17:20–23)

In effect, the key to the author's message is to engage with Jesus as Logos/ Wisdom and that really means to engage with God as light and life, food and nourishment. Vestiges and sometimes very valuable historical information are to be found in this Gospel, but its effect overall is to turn the stories and sayings generated by memory and reflection on the historical

Jesus into a timeless ahistorical symbol of God and God's offer of a relationship of love and life, eternal life. Jesus all but disappears in the process
and becomes an aspect of God's being, a window on God, a mirror of
the divine. This is what one would expect in the way the author reframes
Jesus as God's Wisdom/Word.

Jesus the Word Who Was with God and Was God, an Evolving Conundrum

What began as in part a neat pedagogical ploy to turn badly behaving
men to God by suggesting they fall in love not with wicked women but
with Woman Wisdom became over time a myth or story of Woman Wisdom, an aspect of God. Thus, Wisdom was seen as God's companion and
collaborator, initiating change and hope and identified, as a natural pro-
gression of thought, with the expression of God's will especially as represented in the law. Transposed to apply to Jesus, it cast him as that Wisdom
and Word, making him one with the essence of God, not a second god
like God, but an aspect of God's being. The bi-unity of Wisdom and God
in Jewish tradition became the tri-unity of Father, Son, and Holy Spirit
in Christian affirmation, the Trinity. The myth generated on the margins
became the center of Christian faith.

This development was not without its problems. The author of John's
Gospel would have known that he was engaged in creative symbolism and
fictional dialogues and discourses in his effort to portray what he saw as
the main significance of Jesus. What if his readers and hearers took him
literally? How could Jesus survive this elevation? Could he still be Jesus, the
man from Galilee? How could he be both: God and man? Were there other
ways of saying what the author wanted to say without creating such apparently impossible contradictions? Among the ways were moves to deny
Jesus his place in reality and, instead, to paint him as not human at all but
as a divine figure who had come to rescue people from the harsh realities of
human existence which were the work of a deviant god. Our next chapter
examines the fate of Jesus as this path was followed.

5

The Myth of the Wicked God

THE MYTH OF THE Wicked God is a myth that never made it to the center. It put the blame for so much suffering in creation on the creator, portrayed as a treacherous deity betraying the will of the one and only true God, and out of spite making the mess we find ourselves in: not creating out of chaos, but creating the chaos of creation, an act of ill will. Could people really think like that? Indeed, they could.

Get us out of here! People living in relative comfort, like, I assume, most fellow readers of this book and its author, find it hard to imagine, but for some people then and now, life is hell. Bodies plagued by sores, wracked with pain, malnourished, beaten by abusers, enslaved by "big" people—life here is not worth living. Sadly, for some, suicide beckons. For others, life is simply a struggle, an uphill struggle. Poverty is still a living death for millions, out of sight and out of mind, not least because, malnourished, they lack the energy to protest or to do so in a way that might excite the media.

Modern media and methods make it possible these days to make a difference and wealth creation among the middle classes sometimes trickles down to new possibilities of employment for the poor, though leaving many behind. This is dramatically illustrated, for instance, in recent decades by millions being lifted out of extreme poverty in India and China. Such was not the case in the ancient Mediterranean world of Christian beginnings. There was no media to speak of as we know it. Sickness or disability meant poverty and suffering was largely in silence.

This was the context of the cries for change, calls for divine intervention, engagement in armed rebellion, and, not least, for odd and exceptional charismatic prophets like Jesus of Nazareth, who represented in word and deed the yearning of so many for good news for the poor, a yearning hard to sustain in the movement he engendered.

Apportioning the Blame

For many, such as those sufficiently well-nourished to have the energy for reflective thought and for those deliberately thinking in solidarity with the poor though themselves relatively well off and educated such as temple priests, the basis of hope was divine intervention or at least life beyond the grave. Their hope was especially for a day of judgement when God would set things right and destroy the demons which were making life hell for so many. Blame, as they saw it, belonged sometimes to human beings themselves, including past generations, but especially to the demons let loose upon the world. It was good to be able to exorcize demons from plagued individuals. Jesus and others did it. Hope was for the exorcism of demons from the whole and the beginnings of a new heaven and earth, the coming of God's reign, the kingdom of God. Such hope meant one could hold on, support one another on what for many was the dangerous and depressing journey of human existence.

For others, however, these explanations were not enough. Yes, human sinfulness and the vicious hidden powers plaguing humanity needed to be taken seriously, but the real blame lay deeper. How could it make sense to believe there was a god in control of creation who seemed so oblivious to suffering? How could it make sense to believe there was a god who seemed so selective in deciding on miraculous interventions and then only if sufficiently pestered in prayer and who seemed otherwise to delight in triggering earthquakes, fires and famine? Creation of the material world itself was to blame and, above all, its creator. Creation cannot have been an act of benevolence. It was the doing of a perverse mind, an evil deity, not the true God.

Accompanying this complaint was usually the belief that in each human being there is a spark of light, a spark of the divine. That was what made such thinking and self-awareness possible. This spark of light belonged to the divine but had become trapped by the malicious conspiracy of this angry, perverse god. We are all divine sparks of light trapped in bodies in a physical world designed to plague us. That perverse god is to blame. Hope is to learn that this is so, to have this knowledge, sometimes designated by its Greek word, *gnosis*.

There were numerous speculations about what initiated the divine spat that put this deity offside and created our chaos. Some of them reflect the self-indulgence of the intellectuals of the day with lists of sparring deities, but all of them blame the creator. The creator of this world was malevolent and evil, and we are trapped in our cages of physicality.

We are not used to thinking in this way. What if behind the universe is not a beneficent but a malevolent power or even an indifferent one or nothing and no one? What does such a diagnosis do to our well-being, let alone our hope? Coming on top of the afflictions felt by so many, such a notion crushes the spirit. Believers in the myth of a malevolent creator had one hope: they could hold fast to their connection with the light and so with the God of light, the true God. They would be rescued and so need not give up.

Sometimes this belief comes to us in speculative and abstract stories and explanations penned by reflective thinkers. Sometimes it appears generated by anger and fury. Knowing that anger is usually a feeling that comes second, hard on the heels of a first feeling of pain or hurt, we can empathize with the peddlers of this myth. People were seeking to make sense of their experience and for many that experience was so awful. We need to listen at least to their pain and to those who still endure it today.

Many streams of thought could feed such desperate speculation. Plato's philosophy suggested that the material reality was but the shadow of the genuine heavenly reality and that the soul belonged above but found itself in our bodies as a tomb. Ancient speculation of Persian philosophies saw life as a constant battle between light and darkness.

In addition, some versions of the myth drew directly on Jewish tradition. They rewrote the myths of Genesis to depict Israel's god as the evil creator responsible for the treachery of creation of matter, entrapping our sparks of light, an evil god, not the true God. The snake in the garden of Eden knew that and told Adam and Eve. The Wisdom myth which we discussed in the last chapter could be repurposed so that it now told of the Wisdom of the true God, who could bring us that knowledge, to rescue us from this prison which holds us. Perhaps it was those areas like Idumea, forcibly Judaized by the growing Jewish state in the late second century BCE, which encouraged such anti-Jewish sentiment. In deliberately turning Jewish tradition upside down it could blame Israel's God for not only their state of oppression under Jewish rule but also for the oppressiveness of the material world as a whole.

What then do you do with your material body? Some suggest it meant to do what you like, go wild and enjoy it while you can. More commonly, it meant the opposite. Discipline it. Even punish it. Fast sometimes. Don't follow its whims. You need to eat and drink but never overindulge. And as far as sex is concerned, either suppress it or keep it purely functional. Those who believed in a world to come of transformed non-physical bodies with no sex, originally because it would be a sacred realm, could easily rationalize their sexual suppression: they were seeking to live in the present as they would then. Such beliefs could develop a misogynist tendency, at least to the degree that women could be seen as co-conspirators with the evil creator by reproducing the material species and so perpetuating the entrapment of divine light. Sex was the evil deity's tool of imprisonment.

Hope and relief is to know, to have the *gnosis*, that this is why life is so unbearable and to trust that with that knowledge your spark of light will return to its divine home in God. Such was the message of those who promoted this insight through writing and through support groups of various kinds where likeminded people felt comfort. Could it also help the emerging Jesus movement as it encountered impoverished and plagued humanity? Indeed, it did.

Jesus to the Rescue!

It is not really surprising that some Christ believers came to use traditional titles of Jesus like Redeemer and Savior in new ways. Especially since the belief became established that Jesus was the incarnation or embodiment of Wisdom/Logos, it seemed to many to make sense to claim that he came not just to save people from sin but also to rescue people from their entrapment in the material physical world with a message of hope. People could know that their trapped light would return to the true God.

There were many variations of these thoughts about Jesus. Underlying them all is the message that he came from the world of light from the true God and came to bring knowledge, *gnosis*, to people. To believe in him, to join oneself to him in faith, sometimes, in an echo of the Wisdom myth, to marry or be joined to him, was salvation. The famous text, John 3:16, "For God so loved the world that he gave his only Son that whoever believes in him may not perish but have eternal life," could be read saying precisely that: the true God sent his Son so that we could know how to escape our entrapment in the prison and chaos of the material world. Or, as John 1:9 put it: "The true light, which enlightens everyone, was coming into the world."

Thus, such movements could take up statements about Jesus especially in the highly imaginative Gospel according to John and so hear Jesus' claims in this light. Accordingly, he was, indeed the light, the life, the true bread. Others went further and supplemented the story of Jesus in the Gospels, because, as it stood, that story had made no such claim about Jesus' message and mission. Indeed, giving people knowledge, *gnosis*, by telling them that they came from the light and could return to the light is not how the Gospels portray Jesus' message. "Oh, but yes, it was," became the claim, "and some of disciples knew it!" Supplementing the story of Jesus took the form of describing how Jesus gave such information in secret to select disciples, not Peter, the hero of the established churches which rejected such beliefs, but others named or unnamed.

Already John's Gospel had used this technique to justify its imaginative portrayal by claiming that it came through a figure it called the beloved disciple, probably intending that the inquisitive should identify him as John the son of Zebedee. It remained within acceptable limits for most of the churches from the second century onwards. Not many decades after John's Gospel was penned, however, we find new gospels being written which purport to contain secrets Jesus told. The Gospel according to Mary Magdalene suggests that Jesus imparted secret knowledge to Mary about the soul's origin and its means of escape. Bizarrely, another claims special knowledge on the part of Judas Iscariot who knew that he was facilitating Jesus' escape from his material embodiment, undertaken for a limited time in order to convey his message. Gospels emerged attributed to other disciples, like Philip and Thomas. A new kind of Savior was born and so Jesus entered the myth of the evil god as the one who came to save us from him and his awful deeds.

Jesus to Be Rescued!

In the early centuries the church had to grapple with such growing movements and will surely have heard the timeless argument of some church growth movements that numbers must mean validity. They were growing. They must be right! Through a complex process over time and across diverse regions, the church came to reject such movements and their gospels. It decided to settle on those writings which had mostly firmly established themselves in Christ-believing communities, namely the four Gospels and the letters of Paul and of a few others. Together they formed the New Testament which then functioned as a kind of control, called a canon, against which to measure what was true or false. The matter was complex because trends were already well underway which created fertile soil for such movements.

One of the major trends is apparent already in John's Gospel. The author was hardly unaware of his own creativity in elaborating sayings of Jesus into speeches, inspired as he saw himself by the Spirit whom he saw leading him into all truth and imaginatively claiming "the beloved disciple" as his inspiration. His work is like a modern artist's version of what he found in Mark and had perhaps glimpsed in the other two Gospels or heard from them. His achievement was to portray Jesus as Wisdom/Logos incarnate, as God's Son who came to offer what Jews had for long seen the law as offering, namely light and life, bread and truth. Now, as he portrayed it, this offering was exclusively available through Jesus. Through him all people were offered a relationship of faith and love. From a story about a strongly Jewish Jesus in royal messianic terms it became a message of universal transmissibility, born not least out of its adaptation of the Wisdom myth, as we saw in the previous chapter. It was open to everyone.

John's Gospel was not, however, the product of a separate line of information flowing from one of the original disciples not shared with the rest, as some would like to believe, nor claiming to be. It was a work of art written to promote faith and to repeat through every scene basically the same message of the offer of eternal life from God through love. Almost inevitably, however, people read it also differently, taking its artistic strokes as quasi-photographic, reading it literally. The result was and is that people can see the Jesus of John's Gospel as a god or as God in disguise, walking about Galilee and Judea. He only appeared to be a man. In reality, they claimed, he was God or, at least, God's Wisdom/Logos, God's Son, just seeming to be human but not really human at all. He could play with his opponents because he was all-knowing. It made for great irony and entertainment. He just looked like a human being, but that was a disguise.

There was much which seemed to support this view. Miracles became for some the most effective tool for propaganda in the marketplace of competing religions who championed their heroes as gods or god-like. We can see heightening of miracle stories already in Matthew and Luke's rewriting of Mark. By the time John's Gospel was written, a decade or so later, miracles were becoming ever more impressive. What in some instances were symbolic narratives with scarcely a foothold in reality but inspired to some extent by verbal echoes of Old Testament stories of the feats of Elijah, Elisha or Moses, or God, became proofs of divinity. Our God can walk on water, still storms, multiply food, make wine from water, and resuscitate the dead! Even better than your gods!

The trend was increasingly troubling not because of skepticism, which scarcely arose, but because such emphasis on the wow factor did not cohere well with the message of Jesus, For, despite his impressive acts of healing and exorcism, his message did not base its appeal on acts of magic to win adulation but on his claim to be engaging in God's radical reign of love and liberation. The cross, too, did not sit well in such propaganda which reconfigured Jesus in a way to match the wonderworkers, unless it could be seen as just a stunt along the way to the miracle of resurrection.

The discomfit of authors of New Testament writings with such missional propaganda moves is strikingly widespread. Paul has to insist in writing to the Corinthians that the primary mark of the Spirit is love, not wonders and that, without it, claims to the miraculous don't count, most famously expressed in 1 Corinthians 13, the love chapter:

> If I speak in the tongues of mortals and of angels, but do not have love, I am a noisy gong or a clanging cymbal. [2]And if I have prophetic powers, and understand all mysteries and all knowledge, and if I have all faith, so as to remove mountains, but do not have love, I am nothing. [3]If I give away all my possessions, and if I hand over my body so that I may boast, but do not have love, I gain nothing. . . . [13]And now faith, hope, and love abide, these three; and the greatest of these is love. (1 Corinthians 13:1–3, 13)

Similarly, in writing to the Galatians he underlines that the mark or fruit of the Spirit is preeminently love: "the fruit of the Spirit is love, joy, peace, patience, kindness, generosity, faithfulness, [23]gentleness, and self-control" (5:22).

Matthew creatively portrays Jesus as declaring that at the end of time he will confront those who called him "Lord, Lord" and who paraded their miraculous achievements in his name. He would, indeed, disown them if they had missed the main point of his message as set out in the Sermon on the Mount of love for one another and for God: "Not everyone who says to me, 'Lord, Lord,' will enter the kingdom of heaven, but only one who does the will of my Father in heaven. [22]On that day many will say to me, 'Lord, Lord, did we not prophesy in your name, and cast out demons in your name, and do many deeds of power in your name?' [23]Then I will declare to them, 'I never knew you; go away from me, you evildoers'" (Matt 7:21–23).

The author of John's Gospel is even more confronting of such wow-based propaganda. Reviewing people's response to Jesus' miracles, which the author does not doubt, he writes:

"When he was in Jerusalem during the Passover festival, many believed in his name because they saw the signs [miracles] that he was doing. [24]But Jesus on his part would not entrust himself to them [literally: did not believe in them], because he knew all people [25]and needed no one to testify about anyone [literally: man]; for he himself knew what was in everyone [literally: man]" (John 2:23–25). This is an extraordinary statement, taking up language normally use of conversion, "believed in his name," and having Jesus not believe in them. I have chosen to include the literal references to "man" because it is part of the author's technique which joins this episode to what follows where we read: "Now there was [literally: a man,] a Pharisee named Nicodemus, a leader of the Jews. [2]He came to Jesus by night and said to him, 'Rabbi, we know that you are a teacher who has come from God; for no one can do these signs [miracles] that you do apart from the presence of God.' [3]Jesus answered him, 'Very truly, I tell you, no one can see the kingdom of God without being born from above'" (John 3:1–3). The author wanted us to see that Nicodemus is an example of the kind of belief in Jesus of which, according to the author, Jesus would have disapproved. For all his creativity in writing, the author strongly resists depictions of Jesus as primarily a miracle worker recruiting followers by wowing them with signs and wonders.

We find a similar rebuke in John 4:48 where Jesus declares disapprovingly, "Unless you see signs and wonders you will not believe," and later in the feeding of the five thousand where Jesus refuses the adulation of the crowd who seeing the miracle want to acclaim him as prophet and king: "When the people saw the sign that he had done, they began to say, 'This is indeed the prophet who is to come into the world.' [15]When Jesus realized that they were about to come and take him by force to make him king, he withdrew again to the mountain by himself" (John 6:14–15). The author does not doubt the miracle but, as he goes on to show, he wants them to see Jesus as the bread of life, the true manna come down from heaven. They need to have a different mindset, as he said to Nicodemus, to be "born from above" (John 3:3), a whole new start and new way of thinking. Clearly, the author would not want people to read his creative portrayal as material for propaganda and appears to be concerned to counter such faith.

There was an additional danger which related not just to the way miracle propaganda put emphasis in the wrong place. For, combined with the notion of Jesus as Wisdom/Logos, it could lead, as we have seen, to some seeing Jesus as not human at all but only appearing to be so. Some have read the statement in John 1:14 declaring Jesus as the Word/Wisdom became flesh as already addressing this danger. Becoming flesh, a striking claim, would then be underlining that he was real flesh and blood, however problematic such a statement might seem, to which we shall return. The author paints a scene at the cross which more clearly deals with the danger. It reads: "But when they came to Jesus and saw that he was already dead, they did not break his legs. [34]Instead, one of the soldiers pierced his side with a spear, and at once blood and water came out. [35](He who saw this has testified so that you also may believe. His testimony is true, and he knows that he tells the truth)" (John 19:33–35). This is extraordinary in its emphasis on the truth of what someone reported that they saw, a little like the emphasis given to what John the Baptist said or didn't say in 1:20, "He confessed and did not deny it, but confessed, 'I am not the Messiah.'" This is bending over backwards, as it were, to say: this is true, please believe it! Why? Because some did not! In the scene at the cross, what was true was that blood and water came out when the soldier thrust the spear into Jesus. This is what people would have expected when someone was speared. It meant: Jesus had a real human body. He was really human.

It may be that the story about doubting Thomas being invited to finger Jesus' wounds in 20:27 is seeking to make the same point, on the assumption that in resurrection a body retained its signs of damage.

Within the circles where John's Gospel was written there must have been some who were going overboard in what they claimed about Jesus and in the process were calling his humanity into question and suggesting he only appeared to be human. He wasn't really a man. That was his outward shell or disguise. This probably explains the emphasis in 1 John, written by someone in the same circle as John's Gospel and with similar concerns, when he writes: "We declare to you what was from the beginning, what we have heard, what we have seen with our eyes, what we have looked at and touched with our hands, concerning the word of life— [2]this life was revealed, and we have seen it and testify to it, and declare to you the eternal life that was with the Father and was revealed to us" (1 John 1:1–2).

Not just heard and seen, but also touched—a real human Jesus! By the time that work was written there had been a split in the community and some had left, as 2:18–19 tells us, "Children, it is the last hour! As you have heard that antichrist is coming, so now many antichrists have come. From this we know that it is the last hour. ¹⁹They went out from us, but they did not belong to us; for if they had belonged to us, they would have remained with us. But by going out they made it plain that none of them belongs to us" (1 John 2:18–19). Probably among them were those who were claiming that Jesus was not really human, whom the author dubs, from his point of view, "anti-christs" (2:18–19). For of such anti-christs he writes later that they deny that Jesus came in the flesh: "By this you know the Spirit of God: every spirit that confesses that Jesus Christ has come in the flesh is from God, ³and every spirit that does not confess Jesus is not from God. And this is the spirit of the antichrist, of which you have heard that it is coming; and now it is already in the world" (1 John 4:2–3). Further on, he later makes it clear what that faith means we should believe about Jesus: "This is the one who came by water and blood, Jesus Christ, not with the water only but with the water and the blood" (5:6). This echoes the reference to water and blood in the scene in John's Gospel about the cross and seems also to be emphasizing Jesus' humanity, but perhaps also his death as well as his baptism, if water is alluding to the latter.

Jesus and God

It was a struggle to preserve the memory of Jesus as human, especially once people began to speak of him as Logos/Wisdom in existence before his earthly existence. One of the options was to see Jesus as human, but see Christ as separate, namely as the term for his heavenly existence. This led to the suggestion that Christ entered Jesus at his baptism adopting him as a medium and departed from him shortly before his death. An alternative view was that the Jews were tricked into believing they had crucified Jesus, but instead had crucified Simon of Cyrene, the man who carried his cross, and that God had taken Jesus to heaven just before that. In his book on heresies, the famous church father, Irenaeus (late second-century CE) cites Basilides as an advocate of this view about Jesus' death: "He appeared on earth as a man and performed miracles. Thus he himself did not suffer. Rather, a certain Simon of Cyrene was compelled to carry his cross for him. It was he who was ignorantly and erroneously crucified, being transfigured by him, so that he might be thought to be Jesus. Moreover, Jesus assumed the form of Simon, and stood by laughing at them" (Irenaeus, *Against Heresies* 1.24). A variation of this explanation found its way into the Qur'an: "And [for] their saying, 'Indeed, we have killed the Messiah, Jesus, the son of Mary, the messenger of Allah.' And they did not kill him, nor did they crucify him; but [another] was made to resemble him to them. And indeed, those who differ over it are in doubt about it. They have no knowledge of it except the following of assumption. And they did not kill him, for certain. Rather, Allah raised him to Himself" (Qur'an 4:157–58). It was a serious challenge to hold together the memory and tradition about Jesus as a human being and the claims being made, especially about his being also God or God's Son. When Jews spoke about Wisdom and turned it into a myth of Wisdom being like a woman, a companion of God and God's agent, able to act on God's behalf and so also able to bear God's name, there was never any doubt. This was a way of speaking of God, not of a second God, nor of an angel, for it was God's Wisdom. As noted in the previous chapter, this was a kind of binitarian understanding of God, but never as though there were two separate persons.

When the church experts sought to explain the relationship, they, too, resisted saying the Son was of similar substance to the Father, to God, so in effect a second God, but insisted he was of the same substance. In that sense he was, like Wisdom, part of God's essence. That resolved half the problem, the divine side, but it created enormous difficulties on the human side. How could God or part of God become flesh? We can understand why some found the best solution to lie in denying that Jesus was a real human being and reducing him—or perhaps elevating him—to be just an outward appearance, a kind of disguise which God wore in order to communicate with humanity. And we can understand why others chose to retain Jesus' real humanity but have God in the form of Christ/Logos/Wisdom enter him for the last years of his life at his baptism and leave just before his death.

Jesus, the man, prayed to God not as if talking to himself or to partners in a threesome which constituted the Trinity but as if addressing God as other than himself, from whom he came and to whom he would return. You either compromise Jesus' divinity or you compromise his humanity. The church refused to budge on either and so declared in the Chalcedonian Creed of 461 CE that he was truly God and truly man, holding the paradox together without a solution. It remained without a solution, leaving people who tried to go beyond this almost poetic statement of faith wondering about some very basic questions.

If Jesus was God or part of God, however that is understood, does that mean he came fully equipped with knowledge about the universe, its origins, the earth, its creatures, with scientific expertise beyond imagination? Could he have offered information from the heavenly world about the upper realms, its secrets, such as in some literature of the time famous figures like Enoch could do? Such figures were transported into the heavenly realms and, therefore, it was claimed, could reveal secrets of the universe and its future, masters of science. Was Jesus a walking genius, a universal polymath who knew everything even in advance of the best scientific minds and information today?

Clearly, they did not assume this about Jesus, nor that he had it all in his brain but just chose to remain silent. That is neither what they believed nor the way they were using language about Jesus and Wisdom or Logos. We are not properly attuned to their mode of discourse if we take it literally in this way. Statements about Jesus being Logos/Wisdom/Son of God/ God incarnate are nowhere used to claim that Jesus had such detailed knowledge and nowhere does it suggest he had such detailed knowledge. As often observed, in the Gospel which most extensively highlights Jesus coming as Son sent from the Father, John's Gospel, there is no revelation of data, save that through Jesus God offers life. "He has made him known" in 1:18 does not mean that he provided additional information, but rather that he introduced (or reintroduced) God and God's offer of life. They did not portray him as a genius. They portrayed him as a bearer of God's invitation to share God's light and life. John's Gospel especially frequently speaks of him as God's envoy, but never to suggest he came with a portfolio of information to pass on of what he saw and knew from his previous life in heaven. That is not how they saw it.

Some would therefore put all talk of Jesus' existing before his birth as Logos/Wisdom/Son of God in the category of myth. Such talk serves not to argue that this equipped him to be the bearer of secret heavenly information. Rather it serves to affirm something about him and the way he brought people to encounter God. That affirmation related not to what he saw or heard before his birth but to who he was in the one year or perhaps three of his ministry. Statements about the time before his birth function solely as ways of affirming his authority for what he said and did in his ministry and use the medium of time as a device to do so. They are not used to claim more than that.

New Testament writers never give the impression that they thought Jesus had a life of his own beside God in heaven before his earthly existence, as though he made observations, had conversations, or was otherwise busy in some way. He did not exist in that way before his earthly existence. They never talk in that way. All their talk about his preexistence served to underline his connectedness to God during his ministry and to underline the claim that in his ministry he embodied God's presence and offer of life. Never was this seen by them as at the expense of his being a real human being.

When seen in this light, new approaches become possible to the impossible paradox of Jesus being truly God and truly man. Transposed from a mythical framework of time to a framework of space, one could acclaim the divinity of Jesus in his humanity along the lines that he was deeply connected to God in his being. The author of John's Gospel, who mostly uses the envoy model to portray Jesus as the Son sent by the Father to pass on his message (but never as information always as invitation to life in relationship), in fact, occasionally does this. He drops the temporal framework and depicts Jesus as deriving his authority from his constant contact with God on earth. This deviation from his usual framing is evident in John 5: "Jesus said to them, 'Very truly, I tell you, the Son can do nothing on his own, but only what he sees the Father doing; for whatever the Father does, the Son does likewise. [20]The Father loves the Son and shows him all that he himself is doing; and he will show him greater works than these, so that you will be astonished" (John 5:19–20).

When unpacked, this statement in its context is not about a series of action initiatives or conversations, but about the single repeated theme of the Gospel, namely that Jesus is offering God's eternal life to people. The author clearly assumes a unique status for Jesus as he does so, declaring him to be God's one and only Son, but, aside from the authority claimed in that status, never indicates that it makes him privy to more than what he says and does, namely, to act on God's behalf. His use of the divine name, his action in God's name, calling himself the bread, life, light, and truth, is always ultimately a claim primarily about God and what God offers. In that sense, to say that he comes from the heart of God, using time, namely referring to his preexistence, or using space, namely referring to his connectedness with God in depth, effectively say the same thing. The life of God which confronts us in our image of Jesus is God's Word and Wisdom from the beginning of time and in the depth of reality.

Many see his declarations beginning with "I am" as a play on God's reported self-presentation as "I am that I am" at the burning bush with Moses (Exod 3:14) and its use in Isaiah in reference to God as the "I am" (Isa 43:10–13; 48:12). "Before Abraham was, I am" (John 8:58) may do the same, but may just mean "I existed," just as in the story of Jesus' walking on the water, Jesus' words "I am" (John 6:20) might allude to the divine name but could as in Mark simply mean: "It's me" (6:50). Unquestionably, however, John's Gospel presents Jesus as speaking on God's behalf and offering through himself what God offers, namely eternal life. Such daring depictions are open to be misread.

The author of John's Gospel makes many such claims and elevates Jesus into a symbol of the divine which threatens to obscure or overshadow his humanity, but, where he sees such danger, insists that Jesus' humanity is not to be compromised. We might today employ his artistry in different ways that seek to do the same, not with myth, but in claiming that in Jesus or his short term of ministry we find the wisdom of God, who via Jesus' ministry calls us to relationship and partnership and do so without compromising his humanity and, in that mediatorial sense, his divinity. We can affirm that we hear God in Jesus without needing to employ the myth of making him a dual personality. In that sense, we can embrace what the church sought to do in affirming that he was truly man and truly God and in the Trinity without embracing such statements literally. He was Jesus of Nazareth whose work and words we know through traditions preserved and embedded in narratives which authors of faith created. There are enough of these to enable us to see that he presented to us the challenge of God's being and the timeless invitation to share in that being in love and hope, however we express it.

The Myth That Never Made It

The myth of a corrupt creator who made the material out of spite and trapped divine light in the material of his creation, from which we must be saved, never made it, despite early success. Some claims being made by Christ believers were vulnerable to being associated with beliefs and actions which diminished creation, denying Jesus' real humanity and reducing created reality to a dispensable extra to be jettisoned at death and, at most, to be exploited for interim benefit as one passed it by on the pilgrimage to alternate reality. Harsh living conditions over centuries for so many made hope little more than escape. The story of Jesus then becomes a message of promise of life after death. Easter is then taken as the proof despite the fact that people already believed in resurrection and afterlife in Jesus' world. To reduce it all to something that was not even unique to the Christian gospel, namely, belief in life after death and to ignore the original meaning of resurrection, namely that God vindicated Jesus and his message, is an extraordinary reduction of faith. It, in effect, leaves Jesus and his message behind.

It is such a reduction because, as noted, people already believed in post-mortem survival and a day for resurrection and judgement long before Jesus' death and resurrection, so needed no such proof. Making it primarily a proof of the afterlife misses the point and leaves behind its primary significance. For its significance lay in the belief that by this act God vindicated Jesus and his message. That included, not least, his vision of a transformed society, good news for the poor, a vision which over time became mostly too hard to sustain. For life was too hard. A new heaven and new earth, rather than a renewed heaven and earth, meant starting all over again because the mess is irretrievably bad, and so God must start again. Such truncations and distortions of Jesus' message live on among those who espouse the view: Don't worry about climate change. This earth shall pass away.

For others, negative experience of life led not only to hope for a better world but also to engage in journeys of withdrawal from reality into the inner world of the soul. They took refuge thereby in forms of mysticism which could lift them to enter what they sensed was another dimension, like a parallel universe, an internal realm which brought its own fulfillment within themselves amid the unpromising external realities of life. The preferred translation of Jesus' words referring to his active engagement in healing and restoration, "The kingdom of God is among you" (Luke 17:21) became for some "The kingdom of God is within you." For some, hope was reframed as the ascent of the soul within, a foretaste of ascent of the soul at death. At best, the inner vision and the outer vision combined, and the inward journey motivated the outward journey into engagement in live and compassion in the world.

Other alternatives do not generally include embracing the myth of a peeved deity committing treachery against sparks of light and trapping them in matter but tend in the direction of denying any such gods because even the best gods, as commonly conceived, seem too powerless or preoccupied to address human need without the annoying persistence of prayers. Hope in God lies, then, for more self-critical minds, not in seeing God as a distant deity enthroned in courtly splendor needing to be lobbied to interfere in reality with magical interventions in times of need, but as one present in solidarity in joy and pain, creativity and suffering. Such hope finds God and God's loving amid the turbulence and so makes the cross its symbol. In doing so, it defies the myth which sees us all betrayed by a wayward deity and dares to assume divine benevolence in the beginning, in the end and in the midst of life. Of that there is, of course, no proof. Hope chooses the alternative to believe in such love and so create a meaning for living. It pushes the myth back to the margins.

6

Making Sense of Myths

ONE OF THE TWENTIETH century's greatest New Testament scholars, Rudolf Bultmann, writing in German, used the term *Entmythologisierung* to summarize his challenge to biblical interpreters. It translates as: "demythologizing." He first published his challenge in an essay in German in 1941, a theme then brought into wider circulation especially through his book *Jesus Christ and Mythology*, published in 1958. In it he reminds interpreters that we need to take seriously that we no longer live in a three-tiered universe with heaven above, then earth, and a world below earth: hell or the nether regions. This doesn't mean we should discard ancient beliefs. Rather we should take them seriously and seek to extract from them what is transferrable to our own day where the notion of a three-tiered universe has long ago been abandoned.

We might not be surprised to find a young student enthused by an introduction to astronomy asking when Jesus ascended, did he go into orbit or was he beginning a journey through the galaxies and how far would he have traveled by now? The question is, of course, absurd and asking it may well have been intended to expose that. When I see a sporting hero score or do a touchdown and then point one finger to the sky as if to claim divine help or approval, I smile at the thought that someone on the other side of the world is doing the same but pointing in the opposite direction!

We still use "above" and "below" to talk of God, but the geography has long since ceased to work and we mean it metaphorically. God as below makes just as much sense as God as above. Indeed, at the time that Bultmann was issuing his challenge, others were beginning to subvert the traditional image and speak of God as the ground of our being or deep within. "Heaven" used in the plural as "heavens" now refers at most to the sky above, not to what ancient authors imagined was a high-rise heavenly building with different heavens on each floor and God in the penthouse, as it were. Paul's comment about his quasi-mystical ascent to the third heaven in 2 Corinthians 12:2 was not atypical. Some spoke of three, others of seven, others of multiple heavens, each with its allotted angels and tasks.

We do not mean literally what we say when we use the word heaven or heavens. Often in religious language we do not mean literally what we say, especially when our minds and speech are stretched to give expression to religious experience and insight. Another scholar of recent decades who has also taken the world of the New Testament and its differences from us seriously is John Dominic Crossan. One of his most frequently cited cautions is that we should stop imagining that those ancient people were naïve and gullible for believing literally in so many myths, but rather acknowledge that if *we* do so, *we* are the ones who are naïve and gullible. They knew they were myths. This is, indeed, true, at least in part.

They did, however, believe in a three-tiered universe or, at least some of them exposed to Greek intellectual tradition, in the earth as a sphere around which the sun circled, a belief making earth the center of the universe and therefore so hard to relinquish. The three-tiered model was like seeing earth as a very big saucer covered by a dome with scattered lights in the dome and some moving bodies like the moon and the sun and, above it all, some waters able to drip down upon us as rain and joining the waters below. Deep water below, especially for landlocked Israel, meant the prospect of drowning, as did floods, and so was seen as the source of demons.

The story of Jesus' exorcism at Gerasa has the exorcized demons entering a herd of pigs (animals deemed unclean and so fitting bearers for their hosts) and that these then charge down into the deep, a rather long journey if as it appears the Sea of Galilee was meant, some forty-seven kilometers away (Mark 5:1–20). So, Matthew relocates the event to Gadara, thirty three kilometers closer. Such assumptions give meaning to Jesus' walking on the water, superior to the powers which lay therein, as did the exorcism he performed on the weather, rebuking the wind and telling the sea: "Peace, be still!" and so rescuing the disciples from danger (Mark 4:39).

Already these stories should give us pause to reconsider. Just how literally did they take these stories? The question is valid, given the way the stories clearly function at a symbolic level, celebrating Jesus' ability to save people from the powers that threaten them, whether they be fears or guilt. A kind of neo-fundamentalism which wants to read the Bible as authoritative and fitting in with our assumptions will try to claim that the authors never believed these stories literally. The evidence suggests otherwise. They could take them literally and symbolically at the same time and this is the case with many such stories. As we have seen, the Gospel writers and also Paul were unhappy with focusing just on the literal, which was turning the movement for some into just another sect seeking to wow people to belief with signs and wonders.

If the notion of a three-tiered universe was their widespread understanding of space, there was also something rather more specific in relation to time. The Jesus movement emerges within streams of Judaism that were hoping and expecting major divine intervention in the near future. For John the Baptist the axe was already at the foot of the tree (Matt 3:10; Luke 3:9). For Jesus the kingdom of God was at hand (Mark 1:14–15) and some traditions have him declare that it will happen during the lifetime of some of his hearers (Mark 9:1). Of course, fundamentalists and neo-fundamentalists do their best to explain such statements away, but the integrity of respecting and acknowledging difference, even when it may be uncomfortable, is to be preferred. It makes the process of demythologizing cleaner.

Paul, too, shared this view of time, expecting that he would still be alive when Jesus would return as part of that divine intervention: "For the Lord himself, with a cry of command, with the archangel's call and with the sound of God's trumpet, will descend from heaven, and the dead in Christ will rise first. [17]Then we who are alive, who are left, will be caught up in the clouds together with them to meet the Lord in the air; and so we will be with the Lord for ever" (1 Thessalonians 4:16–17). He expresses the same expectation in 1 Corinthians 15:51–52. The reason why the movement did not collapse when such expectations failed to be realized was that the fundamental concerns of the movement lay not with particular notions of space or timing but with direct encounter with God.

Not just the framework of a three-tiered universe populated by demons and the failed expectations in relation to timing needed demythologizing. The myths and stories themselves created within that universe need demythologizing. That calls for critical thought, including self-critical thought. The myth of lusting angels coming down to have sex with women and so producing giants makes little sense for us. We have relegated giants to fairy stories, such as "Jack and the Beanstalk."

With the next episode, namely the giants' demise and the emergence of the sickness and other demons, we recognize a primitive scientific advance. We don't personalize viruses and call them demons, but it makes sense to us, too, to see illness not necessarily as self-inflicted nor as inflicted by God or gods from their divine control center, but as part of the reality with which we must live.

Yes, not personalizing them means we do not attribute to them deliberate strategies to harm, let alone hoping to have them bound and sent to fire on the day of judgement. But we certainly stand with the mythmakers in seeing human welfare threatened by forces sometimes outside their control, whether illness or with them political powers and human structures which dehumanize. The kingdom of God, the reign of God, means liberation from the powers which oppress people.

Beyond that, the myth served as a model of how things can go so very wrong when some boundaries are crossed leading to unforeseen consequences. Some used the myth to warn against all that was deemed unnatural, including sex with other species, but also, based on their assumptions, sex between men and between women instead of between men and women. The assumption that men or women attracted to their own sex were acting contrary to their nature and so were perverts or at best very sick made such conclusions possible, but these, too, like the notion of a three-tiered universe, need updating. Even at a purely physical level some people are born intersex, neither straightforwardly male nor female, but with mixed genitalia. That should alert us to abandon the dogma that claims all humans are heterosexually either male or female and the damaging conclusions which usually accompany it.

Similarly, like "above" and "below" in religious discourse, the language of kingship and power is alive and well in contemporary expression. It still seems more comfortable for many to think of God as a king, enthroned above, exercising power and looking for adulation, than to think of God as loving, generous, engaged in highly and lowly service. Mark's struggle to set things right by rejecting such notions of Jesus have largely fallen on deaf ears and so the myth of divine kingship reigns and continues to offer a model for power and control in the church and beyond about what makes for greatness. So many politicians seem more concerned with self-marketing and hanging on to power than with putting people and their needs first.

The solution is not to deny power, let alone bedevil it. Those who pretend not to have power or who fail to acknowledge the power they have are frequently a danger to themselves and society. So, the traditional language of kingship was acknowledging something, even if in most countries monarchies are defunct or reduced to symbolism. Jesus had power, however he understood it, and exercised it within the framework of understanding people and how to help them in his day. He proclaimed God's reign, the kingdom of God. That's a claim to power, God's power. But the sayings and stories preserved from his short year or so of ministry make it very clear that he did not want power for its own sake or his own sake. He was not going about seeking adulation. As Luke has Peter report in his speech to Cornelius and his gentile friends, "he went about doing good and healing all who were oppressed by the devil, for God was with him" (Acts 10:38). He recruited others to join him in doing the same. His resurrection was not the glory he sought for himself all along to be earned by doing good, but God's declaration that what he did was exactly what God wanted and what is also God's priority. The author of 1 John captured it well in twice repeating: "God is love" (4:8, 16).

Humanity, or at least powerful human beings, created God in their image as great because he had power and was like one of their kings and even greater. That image then went on to reinforce their values. Royal court ideology hijacked spirituality for many and our liturgies and hymn-books bear witness to its influence. It was very hard to hear the acclamation of Jesus as the Christ, let alone, Jesus as Lord, as meaning anything other than that his agenda is glory and adulation. Washing the disciples' feet as depicted in John 13 is then an aberration not an example and the crucified king, enthroned on a cross bearing a crown of thorns, no more than Roman ridicule.

Accordingly, the now diverse and broad stream of Christian tradition bears along within it both good news and bad, liberation and oppression, health and harm. Dams and treatment plants are no longer possible. Critical reflection, however, is possible and needed more than ever.

The myth of Woman Wisdom, brainchild in part of a moral educator, is more accessible to us in its focus on relationship and oneness with God and God's law. It transfers well across time and culture. Its rich symbolism of bread, water, light, and life, elements which address basic human needs, works well in depicting God and God's wisdom as nourishment and enlightenment for life. As such, the myth still speaks even without its mythical notions of descent from above. It is bigger than a Christian concept. It is fundamentally Jewish, but easily adapted to be a universal image of the divine.

In the hands of Christ followers it finds itself merged with traditions in ways that both enlighten and obscure and even sometimes obfuscate. It was a winsome way to shift from the Jewish nationalist hope for a royal messianic Son of God and king like David, however redefined, to fit Jesus. For it could take up the story couched in royal messianic terms, which saw Jesus' resurrection as enthronement to come as king and then as ruling from the heavens, and turn it into an acclamation of Jesus to be seen as God's Wisdom or Logos, God's Son, ruling not just in the present and in future but from the beginning of time. It is most developed in the fourth Gospel, where we therefore read of the Word who was with God and was God who came to earth, became flesh and a temple of God's presence, and offered bread, water, light, and life.

The author mostly uses the motif of the envoy who played such a crucial role as bearer of communication in the ancient world and so repeatedly speaks of Jesus or has Jesus speak of himself as the one sent from above. The gospel's first hearers must have recognized the creativity at work in this image because in fact where one might have expected the envoy to communicate information, they hear no such thing. Where fantasy might imagine Jesus as an envoy coming with a portfolio of revelation to offer knowledge of the universe and its workings, indeed, to be the world's best scientist, John says no such thing. Jesus didn't found a university.

This alerts us to the importance of listening to what the author was doing in telling such a story. He was not really using the notion of Jesus existing before his manifestation on earth to make claims about information and shows no interest in taking the story literally in that sense, such as to explain what Jesus had been doing in the previous four thousand years, let alone in the previous 13.5 billion (minus two thousand) years. The purpose of telling such a story of preexistence with no content was to acclaim that in Jesus God and God's Wisdom was present offering light and life, water and bread.

I suspect that if we could ask him, the author would have explained that of course Jesus existed before his birth on earth but not as one would normally understand it. Rather, he would explain, the point of telling such a story is to say that the Jesus of his Gospel presented God. The myth of Woman Wisdom, adapted to a male form, as God's eternal Word, was a way of declaring his Jesus to be that voice of God. The myth, so adapted, enabled him to make that claim. It was not about a Jesus waiting around for millennia to engage on his mission.

We need to enter the mindset of those sages, who speculated that people and events were loaded to go, as it were, in the heavenly realms, like the author of the book of Revelation sees a scroll of human history gradually being unrolled (Revelation 5). That was the model for preexistence, the rationale for the myth of origin of significant people and events. Was it all thought through with clear differentiation between what was symbolic and what was not? Most likely not. At most we need to observe what a story or myth was doing more than what it was saying.

What the story of the Word becoming flesh was saying created enormous difficulties. Little wonder the author found himself having to work hard to hold onto the memory of Jesus as being a real human being and not a charade or fantasy. What he was doing was making a claim about Jesus. What he was saying made it sound like Jesus was a god in disguise playing with his dialogue partners whose failure to understand added a kind of entertainment value for his hearers who knew the inside story. The matter became even more complicated because of the author's extensive creativity in making up dialogues which, taken at face value, really could sound like Jesus was not really human. His adaptation, extrapolation, and embellishment of sayings and stories of Jesus now all serve to repeat the same melody, the same message, that he came to offer God's eternal life, is at times quite brilliant. He could use irony, misunderstanding, and unreal stage characters larger than life to engage his audience.

That creativity, for all its worth in returning to the fundamental values and function of the Wisdom myth, acerbated a problem he keenly realized, namely the notion that Jesus was not a flesh and blood human who died fully human, bleeding blood and water from a spear thrust as you would expect from any other human. The author of 1 John, as we have seen, sought to reaffirm his humanity, but too late for some who must have misread the gospel.

What began simply, became something of a mess and in time combined with the negativity of those who had concluded that this material creation was a nasty piece of doing, produced by a renegade god. Those who combined the myth of the renegade god with their faith in Christ, of course, denied he could have in any way been human and have been like the rest of us trapped in the material world. He was instead the Redeemer, the Liberator, come to awaken in us the knowledge and memory that our spark of light so trapped could escape and find its way back to the divine.

Combining core insight and complex imagery, the church refused to surrender Jesus' humanity to such devotion. It refused to surrender the claim that he bore God's life to the world, employing the insights of the Wisdom myth to declare him like Wisdom one with and in God like God's Spirit and so held at bay all options which denied that Jesus was truly God and truly human. It was a weaving together of myth and history, but one which sounded blasphemous for Jew and Muslim alike for what it said. There are better prospects for understanding when we consider what it did and better ways of saying it without the entanglement in myth. That means a retelling in which we tell our own story and employ our own myths while seeking to be faithful to what in all it did.

Myths mask meaning in story and sometimes those meanings are profound. Sometimes they are misleading. Myths are not "false" as though myth is the opposite of truth. Myth, especially in the ancient world, was a way of seeking to say why things are the way they are. In that sense they tell the truth or seek to do so. Translating myths means first listening to them, hearing what their stories are really saying. It is like visiting an art gallery not to see photographs, but to see images, knowing that images sometimes say it more powerfully than photographs. The ancient writers clothed truth in art sometimes in ways that enhance in us a sense of distance because we no longer share many of their assumptions about earth, the universe, and humanity. That, then, makes us all the more aware of what we do share and so the distance we experience also creates proximity and helps us engage.

Sometimes their truths and aspirations will be far from ours in much more than a historical sense. Sometimes, however, we will feel uncomfortably at home because they speak to us. Some must never be at the center. Some will always be there, like the myth of glorious kingship subverted in the cross, like wisdom as the heart of God, and like the ongoing story of love's confrontation of oppressive powers and its message of liberation. We can make sense of myths if we try, and myths can then make sense of us and for us.

Bibliography

The Bible. New Revised Standard Version containing the Old and New Testaments with the Apocryphal / Deuterocanonical Books. New York: Oxford University Press, 1989.

The Qur'an. https://legacy.quran.com/4/157-158.

Charlesworth, James H., ed. *The Old Testament Pseudepigrapha*. 2 vols. New York: Doubleday, 1983–85.

Colson, F. H., and G. H. Whitaker, trans. *Philo in Ten Volumes (and Two Supplementary Volumes)*. 12 vols. Loeb Classical Library. London: Heinemann, 1929–62.

Fitzmyer, Joseph A. *The Genesis Apocryphon of Qumran Cave 1 (1Q20): A Commentary*. 3rd ed. Biblica et Orientalia 18B. Rome: Pontificio Istituto Biblico, 2004.

Hollander, Harm W., and Marinus de Jonge. *The Testaments of the Twelve Patriarchs: A Commentary*. Studia in Veteris Testamenti Pseudepigrapha 8. Leiden: Brill, 1985.

Nickelsburg, George W. E., and James C. VanderKam. *1 Enoch: A New Translation*. Minneapolis: Fortress, 2004.

Tigchelaar, J. C. Eibert. *Prophets of Old and the Day of the End: Zechariah, the Book of Watchers and Apocalyptic*. Oudtestamentische Studiën 35. Leiden: Brill, 1996.

Tov, Emanuel. *The Dead Sea Scrolls Electronic Library*. Leiden: Brill, 2006.

VanderKam, James C., ed. and trans. *The Book of Jubilees: A Critical Text*. 2 vols. Corpus Scriptorum Christianorum Orientalium 510–11. Leuven: Peeters, 1989.